The Political Future of India

The
Political Future of India

by

Lajpat Rai

GYAN

Published by

GYAN

Gyan Publishing House
5, Ansari Road
Daryaganj, New Delhi-110002
Phone: 011-47034999, 9811692060
E-mail: books@gyanbooks.com

Distribution Network
gyanbooks.com
India, USA, Canada, UK, Australia, France

ISBN: 978-81-212-7993-2 (PB)
First Published, 1921

2nd Impression 2023

Printed at: Gyan Press, Delhi.

THE POLITICAL FUTURE OF INDIA
Author: LAJPAT RAI

The Political Future of India

The Political Future of India

by

Lajpat Rai

NEW YORK
B. W. HUEBSCH
MCMXIX

TO MY FRIEND

COLONEL JOSIAH WEDGWOOD, M. P., D. S. O.

PREFACE

My book, *Young India*, was written during the first year of the war and was finally revised and sent to the press before the war was two years old. It concluded with the following observation:

"The Indians are a chivalrous people; they will not disturb England as long as she is engaged with Germany. The struggle after the war might, however, be even more bitter and sustained."

The events that have happened since have amply justified the above conclusion. India not only refrained from disturbing England while she was engaged in war with Germany, but actively helped in defeating Germany and winning the war. She raised an army of over a million combatants and supplied a large number of war workers, and made huge contributions in money and materials. She denied herself the necessities of life in order to feed and equip the armies in the field though within the last months of the war when scarcity and epidemic overtook her, she lost six millions of her sons and daughters from one disease alone — influenza. This was more than chivalry. This was self-effacement in the interests of an Empire which, in the past, had treated her children as helots. How much of this effort was voluntary and how much of it was forced it is difficult to appraise. Great Britain, however, has unequivocally accepted it as voluntary and has attributed it to India's satisfaction with her rule. That India was not satisfied with her rule she has spared no pains to impress upon the British people as well as the rest of the world. Reading between the lines of the report of the Secretary of State for India and the Viceroy has established the fact of that dissatisfaction beyond the possibility of doubt, but if any doubt still remained it has been dispelled by the writings and utterances of her representative spokesman in India, in Great Britain and abroad. The prince and the peasant, the landlord and the ryot, the professor and the student, the politician and the layman — all have spoken. They differ in their estimates of the "blessings" of British rule, they differ in the manner of their profession of loyalty to the British Empire, they sometimes differ in shaping their schemes for the future Government of India but they are all agreed:

(1) That the present constitution of the Government of India is viciously autocratic, bureaucratic, antiquated and unsatisfying.

(2) That India has, in the past, been governed more in the interests of, and by the British merchant and the British aristocrat than in the interests of her own peoples.

(3) That the neglect of India's education and industries has been culpably tragic and–

(4) That the only real and effectual remedy is to introduce an element of responsibility in the Government of India.

In the report of the Secretary of State and the Viceroy, so often quoted and referred to in these pages, the truth of (1), (3), and (4) is substantially admitted and point (2) indirectly conceded. In the following pages an attempt is made to prove this by extracts from the report itself. Ever since the report was published in July, 1918, India has been in a state of ferment, — a ferment of enthusiasm and criticism, of hope and disappointment. While the country has freely acknowledged the unique value of the report, the politicians have differed in their estimates of the value of the scheme embodied therein. Yet there is a complete unanimity on one point, that nothing *less* than what is planned in the report will be accepted, even as the first step towards eventual complete responsible Government. This is the minimum. Even the ultra-moderates have expressed themselves quite strongly on that point. Speaking at the Conference of the Moderates held at Bombay on November 1, 1918, the President, Mr. Surendranath Banerjea, is reported to have said: "our creed is co-operation with the Government wherever practicable, and opposition to its policy and measures when the supreme interests of the mother-land require it. . . . I have a word to say . . . to the British Government. I have a warning note to sound. . . . If the enactment of the Reform proposals is unduly postponed, if they are whittled down *in any way* . . . there will be grave public discontent and agitation." A little further in the same speech he asked if "by the unwisdom of our rulers" India was "to be converted into a greater Ireland." In less than six months from the date of this pronouncement, the rulers of India gave ample proof of their "unwisdom" by actually converting India into a "greater Ireland" and in establishing the absolute correctness of the prognostication made by the present writer in the concluding sentence of his book *Young India.* The manifesto of the Moderate Party issued over the signatures of the Moderate leaders all over the country contained the following warning: "We must equally protest against every attempt, by whomever made and in whatever manner, at any mutilation of the Montagu-Chelmsford proposals. We are constrained to utter a grave warning against the inevitable disastrous effects of such a grievous mistake on the future relations of the British Government and the Indian people which will result in discontent and agitation followed by repression on the one side and suffering on the other side." Little did they know when they uttered the warning that repression would come even before the Reform Scheme was discussed in Parliament and "mutilated" there. British rule in Ireland has been for the last twenty years a wearisome record of mixed concessions and coercions. Every time a concession was made it was either preceded or accompanied by strong doses of coercion. One would have thought that British statesmen were wiser by their experience of Ireland, but it seems that they have learnt nothing and that they have no intention of doing in India anything different from what they have been doing in Ireland. The history of British statesmanship in relation to Irish affairs is repeating itself almost item by item in India.

Lord Morley's reforms were both preceded and followed by strong measures of repression and suppression. As if to prove that British statesmanship can never in this respect set aside precedent even for once, Mr. Montagu's proposals have been followed by a measure of coercion unique even for India. Mr.

Montagu's proposals for the reconstruction of Government in India are yet in the air. They are being criticised and examined minutely by numerous British agencies both in India and in England as to how and in what respects they can be made innocuous. Certain other reforms promised by the report, such as the scheme for Local Self Government and the policy in relation to the Arms Act, have already been disposed of in the usual masterly way of giving with one hand and taking back with the other. Similarly the "great" scheme of opening the commissioned ranks of the Army to the native Indians has practically (for the present at least) ended in fiasco. But the policy underlying the Rowlatt laws has surpassed all. In the chapters of this book dealing with the Revolutionary movement the reader will find a genesis of the Rowlatt laws of coercion.

On the sixteenth of January in the *Gazette of India* was published a draft of two bills that were proposed to be brought before the Legislative Council of India (which has a standing majority of Government officials). These bills were to give effect to the recommendations of the committee presided over by Mr. Justice Rowlatt of the High Court of England, for the prevention, detection and punishment of sedition in India. Their introduction into the Legislative Council was at once protested against by all classes of Indians with a unanimity never before witnessed in the history of India. All sections of the great Indian population from the Prince to the peasant, including all races, religions, sects, castes, creeds and professions joined in the protest. Hindus, Mohammedans, Indian Christians, Sikhs, Buddhists, Parsees — all stood up, to a man, to oppose the measure. All the political parties, Conservatives, Liberals, Moderates and Extremists expressed themselves against it. The measure was opposed by all the non-official Indian members of the Legislative Council. All methods of agitation were resorted to in order to make the opinion of the country known to the Government and to warn the latter against the danger of defying the united will of the people. The press, the pulpit and the platform all joined in denouncing the measures, meetings of protest were held in all parts of the country and resolutions wired to the Government. A few days before the final meeting at which these bills were to be passed into law a number of prominent citizens, male and female, pledged themselves to passive resistance in case the measures were enacted. The passive resistance movement was inaugurated and led by Mr. M. K. Gandhi, a man of saintly character, universally respected and revered in India, the same who stood for the Government during the war and rendered material help in recruiting soldiers, raising loans and procuring other help for its prosecution. The following is the text of the pledge that was signed by hundreds and thousands of Indians belonging to all races and religions and hailing from all parts of the continent:

"Being conscientiously of opinion that the bills known as the Indian Criminal Law (Amendment) Bill No. 1 of 1919 and No. 2 of 1919 are unjust, subversive of the principle of liberty and justice and destructive of the elementary rights of individuals on which the safety of the community as a whole and the State itself is based, we solemnly affirm that, in the event of these bills becoming law, we shall refuse civilly to obey these laws and such other laws as a committee to be hereafter appointed may think fit and we further affirm that in this struggle we will faithfully follow truth and refrain from violence of life, person or property."

The passive resistance movement was not approved by the country as a whole, and influential voices were raised against it even in its early stages but the fact that Mr. Gandhi had taken the responsibility of initiating and leading it and that many women had signed the pledge should have opened the eyes of the Government as to the intensity of the feeling behind it. Besides this threat of passive resistance the Indian members of the Council showed their solid opposition to the measure by using all the historic obstructive methods so well known to the student of Parliamentary debates in the House of Commons as associated with the Irish Nationalist party under the leadership of Parnell. The debates in the Legislative Council of India do not ordinarily last for more than one day, consisting, at the most, of eight hours. The debate on this bill lasted for three days; one sitting lasted "from 11 o'clock in the morning . . . until nearly half past one the following day with adjournments for luncheon and dinner." The officials were determined to pass the bill at that sitting and so they refused to rise until the amendments on the agenda had been disposed of and the bill passed into law. The non-officials proposed no less than 160 amendments but by the application of closure methods they were all disposed of in three days and the bill passed (on the 18th of March). The Government made a few minor concessions but on the whole the bill remained as it had been drafted, a monument of Governmental shortsightedness and stupidity. The consideration of the other bill was postponed. As soon as the news reached Bombay that the first bill had become law "the market was closed as a protest" and posters in English and the vernacular, were displayed throughout the city urging the non-payment of taxes and asking the people to resist the order of a tyrannical Government." (London *Times*, April 2.) Similar manifestations of anger were made throughout the country and the movement for passive resistance was definitely inaugurated. It spread like wild fire. Thousands joined it and the relations between the people and the Government became very strained. However, no violence was resorted to, nor was any harm done to life and property. Several members of the Legislative Council resigned their offices. One of them a Mohammedan leader, wrote the following letter to His Excellency the Viceroy:

"Your Excellency, the passing of the Rowlatt Bill by the Government of India and the assent given to it by your Excellency as Governor-General against the will of the people has severely shaken the trust reposed by them in British justice. Further, it has clearly demonstrated the constitution of the Imperial Legislative Council which is a legislature but in name, a machine propelled by a foreign executive. Neither the unanimous opinion of the non-official Indian members, nor the entire public opinion and feeling outside has met with the least respect. The Government of India and your Excellency, however, have thought it fit to place on the statute-book a measure admittedly obnoxious and decidedly coercive at a time of peace, thereby substituting executive for judicial discretion. Besides, by passing this Bill, your Excellency's Government have actively negatived every argument they advanced but a year ago when they appealed to India for help at the War Conference, and have ruthlessly trampled upon the principles for which Great Britain avowedly fought the war.

"The fundamental principles of justice have been uprooted and the constitutional rights of the people have been violated, at a time when there is no real danger to the state, by an overfearful and incompetent bureaucracy which is neither responsible to the people, nor in touch with real public opinion and their whole plea is that 'powers when they are assumed will not be abused.'

"I, therefore, as a protest against the passing of the Bill and the manner in which it was passed, tender my resignation as a member of the Imperial Legislative Council, for I feel that, under the prevailing conditions, I can be of no use to my people in the Council, nor, consistently with one's self respect, is coöperation possible with a Government that shows such utter disregard for the opinion of the representatives of the people in the Council Chamber and the feelings and sentiments of the people outside.

"In my opinion, a Government that passes or sanctions such law in times of peace forfeits its claim to be called a civilized Government and I still hope that the Secretary of State for India, Mr. Montagu, will advise his Majesty to signify his disallowance to this Black Act.

"Yours truly,

"M. A. Jinnah."

The leaders of the passive resistance movement declared 30th March as "the National protest day." The protest was to be made by all the traditional methods known to India for ages, viz., by fasting, stopping business, praying, and meeting in congregations in their respective places of worship. The only Western method contemplated was passing resolutions and sending telegrams to the authorities in India and England. The 30th of March was thus observed as a national protest day throughout India and there was only one clash between the people and the Government, viz., at Delhi, the national capital.

Delhi has been the national capital of India from times immemorial. It was the chief capital city of the Moguls. It has a mixed population of Hindus and Mohammedans, almost evenly divided. The European population there is not very large. There is a British garrison stationed in the Mogul fort. Besides being the capital of British India, Delhi is a very important trade center and the terminus of several railway lines. All business was stopped, shops closed and the city gave an appearance of a general strike. A mass meeting attended by 40,000 people, according to British estimates, and presided over by a religious ascetic, passed resolutions of protest and cabled them to the Secretary of State for India in London. It was at Delhi and on this day as already stated that the first clash occurred between the authorities and the people. It is immaterial how it came about but it may be noted that rifles and machine guns were freely used in dispersing the mobs at the railway station and other places. According to official estimates fourteen persons were killed and about sixty wounded. The non-official estimates give larger figures. Evidently nothing serious happened between March 30th and April 6th which last was observed as a day of mourning throughout British India from Peshawar to Cape Comorin and from Calcutta to Karachi and Bombay. People held meetings, made speeches, marched in processions, took pledges of passive resistance, closed shops, suspended business, bathed in the sea, joined in prayer and fasted. No violence of any kind was reported. In the words of a correspondent of the London *Times*, "the distinguishing feature of many of these demonstrations [meaning thereby passive resistance demonstrations] made on the 6th of April, specially at Delhi, Agra, Bombay and Calcutta, is the Hindu and Moslem fraternization, Hindus being freely admitted to the mosques, on occasions occupying the Mihrab (the niche indicating the direction of Mecca)." In a message dated April 7th the same correspondent cabled "an unprecedented event in the shape of a joint Moslem-Hindu service at the famous Juma Masjed at Delhi, at which a Hindu[1] delivered a sermon." The Juma Masjed is one of the jewels of Mogul architecture and probably the biggest mosque in India.

On April 9th Sir Michael O'Dwyer, the Lieutenant Governor of the Punjab, dwelt with pride on the fact that the province ruled by him with an iron hand for the last five years "had raised 360,000 combatants during the war." "Dealing with the political situation he declared that the Government of the province was determined that public order which was maintained during the war, should not be disturbed during peace. Action had therefore been taken under the Defence Act against certain individuals who were openly endeavoring to arouse public feeling against the Government." It was this action, viz., the sum-

[1] This Hindu happened to be the leader of a section of the Arya Samaj — an organization known for its bitter attitude towards Mohammedanism.

mary arrest of leaders at Amritsar and the order of prohibition against Mr. Gandhi's contemplated visit to the Punjab, that set fire to the accumulated magazine. It exasperated the people and in a moment of despair the intense strain of the last few weeks found relief in attacks on Government buildings and stray persons of European extraction. What actually happened in different places no one can definitely tell just at this stage but it is clear that at places so widely distant as Amritsar and Lahore in the Punjab and Viramgam in the Gujerat (Western Presidency) railway stations, telegraph offices and some other public buildings were burned, railway traffic interrupted, tram cars stopped and some Europeans killed and attacked. At Amritsar three banks were burnt down and their managers killed. Telegraphing on April 15th and again on the 16th of April, the correspondent of the London *Times* remarked that "the Punjab continued to be the principal seat of trouble" which was probably due to the extremely brutal methods which the Punjab Government had followed in repressing and suppressing not only the present 'riots' but also all kinds of political activity in the preceding six years. It appears that in about a week's time almost the whole province was ablaze. The Government used machine guns in dispersing meetings, showered bombs from aeroplanes and declared martial law in several towns, extended the seditious meetings prevention Act and other emergency laws in districts, marched flying military columns from one end to the other, accompanied by travelling courts martial to try and punish on the spot all arrested for offences committed in connection with the passive resistence movement. Leaders were arrested and deported without trial of any kind; papers were suppressed and all kinds of demonstrations prohibited.

Among the leaders arrested are the names of some of the most conservative and moderate of the Punjab public men — men whose whole life is opposed to extremism of any kind. Those men were subjected to various indignities, handcuffed and marched to jail. They have been held in ordinary prison cells and all comforts have been denied to them as if they were criminals. Counsel engaged for them from outside the Province have been refused admission into the Province. Machine guns and aeroplanes have been used in dispersing unarmed mobs and crowds were fired at in many places. At Lahore the General Officer Commanding gave notice "that unless all the shops were re-opened within 48 hours all goods in the shops not opened will be sold by public auction." As to the causes of the upheaval, the Anglo-Indian view is contained in a telegraphic message to the London *Times* bearing date April 20th. Below we give a verbatim copy of this message:

CAUSES OF THE UPHEAVAL.

"Bombay, April 20. — We have passed through the most anxious ten days that India has known for half a century. We have further anxious days in store, for although in Bombay conditions are improving and Mr. Gandhi has publicly abandoned the passive resistance movement, while men of weight are rallying to the support of the Government, the situation in Northern India is disquieting.

"We may pause to enquire into this widespread manifestation of violence. How came it that passive resistance to the Rowlatt Act — never likely to be applied to the greater part of India, especially to

Bombay, and nominally confined to the sale of proscribed literature of doubtful legality, which was waning — suddenly flamed into riot, arson, and murder at Delhi, Ahmedabad, Viramgam, Amritsar, and other parts of the Punjab on the prevention of Mr. Gandhi's entry into Delhi? All day on April 11 Bombay stood on the brink of a bloody riot, averted only by the Governor, Sir George Lloyd's prudent statesmanship and the great restraint of the police and military in face of grave provocation.

"The movement seems to have been twofold. In part it was the expression of the prevailing ferment. India is no less affected than other parts of the world by the social and intellectual revolution of the war, by expectations based on the destruction of German materialism and by ambitions for fuller partnership in the British Empire.

PROFITEERING AND TRICKERY.

"The disruptive effect of these ideals is accentuated by prevailing conditions. The prices of food are exceedingly high, supplies are scanty, while efforts to control prices are hampered by the profiteering and trade trickery unfortunately never absent from this country. [As if it was absent from other countries.]

"India having been swept bare of foodstuffs, to meet the exigencies of the war, the people feel that the home Government is lukewarm in releasing supplies from outside, and resent particularly that the Shipping Controller is maintaining high freights on fat and rice from Burma. These severe sufferings are superimposed on the devastating influenza and cholera epidemics. So much for the social and economic situation.

"Then the activities of the Indo-British Association created grave doubts whether Parliament will deal fairly with India when the reform scheme is considered. The Rowlatt Act was precipitated into this surcharged atmosphere.

"The Act was wickedly perverted by the Extremists until among the common people it became the general belief that it gave plenary powers to a police which was feared and distrusted. Among educated people, few of whom studied the report or the Act, it was bitterly resented as a badge of India's subjection after loyal participation in the war, at a time when the strongest feeling in the country was craving for its self-respect in the eyes of the nations. Further, it was regarded as prejudicing the cause of political reform.

"Another powerful contributory cause was the ferment amongst the Moslem community. Everywhere the Moslems believe that the Peace Conference is bent on the destruction of Islam. There is no confidence in British protection after our declared policy in regard to Turkey and the undoing of the settled fact in Eastern Bengal in 1911.

"This feeling is the more dangerous because it is inchoate. Moslem officers returned from Palestine and Arabia, and acquainted with the realities of Turkish rule, have expressed astonishment at the strength of this feeling among their co-religionists here. Mohamedans have been foremost in the work of riot and destruction in Ahmedabad and Delhi, and the lower elements were ripe for trouble in Bombay. I am unable to say how far this ferment affected the outbreaks in the Punjab.

"This seething Moslem unrest is the most menacing feature of Indian politics to-day. It explains the unprecedented admission of Hindus to the Mosques of Delhi and Aligarh. . . .

REVOLUTIONARY INSPIRATION

"So much for the general situation. In Northern India the outbreaks were nakedly revolutionary. They are unconnected with the Rowlatt Act or with passive resistance, which probably precipitated a movement long concerted. There is abundant evidence of the organized revolutionary character of the disturbances in the systematic attacks on railways, telegraphs, and all means of communication, and its definitely anti-British character is apparent from the efforts to plunge the railways into a general strike.

"There are signs of the inter-connection of the Punjab revolutionaries with the Bombay revolutionaries who organized attacks on communications at Ahmedabad and Viramgam, derailed trains, cut telegraphs, and sent rowdies from Kaira to take part in the work of destruction. There is evidence also of some outside inspiration, but whether Bolshevist or otherwise is obscure.

"Whilst in the Punjab the soil was fruitful, owing to economic conditions, the ravages of influenza, and the pressure of last year's recruiting campaign, the revolutionary origin of the disturbances is unquestioned. . . ."

As usual the message is a mixture of truth and imagination. At most it is a partisan view. Be the causes what they may, the events in our judgment amply justify the following conclusions:

(*a*) That India is politically united in demanding a far reaching measure of self-determination.

(*b*) That she will not be satisfied with paltry measures of political reform which do not give her power to shape her fiscal policy in her own interests, independent of control from London.

(*c*) That it is useless to further harp on the "cleavages" of race, religion and language, in dealing with the problem of India.

(*d*) That the country is no longer prepared to let measures of coercion pass and take effect without making their protest and dislike known to the authorities in a manner, the significance of which may not be open to misunderstanding.

The Indian members of the Legislative Council while opposing the Rowlatt Bills spoke in sufficiently clear and strong language of the grave situation the Government was creating by its ill-considered policy. They knew their people. The bureaucracy evidently dismissed it as bluff or, if it knew what was likely to happen, encouraged it in the hope that the outbreak might justify their opposition to, and dislike of, the Montagu-Chelmsford scheme. In doing that they have had to hatch the eggs they themselves laid. These events have, besides, proved (*a*) that the lead of the country has passed from the hands of the so called "natural leaders," the aristocracy of land, money and birth; (*b*) that even the moderate leaders have considerably lost in prestige and influence; (*c*) that the lead has definitely passed into hands that openly and frankly stand for self-determination and self-government within the Empire and are prepared for *any sacrifice* to achieve that end; (*d*) that the old methods of governing India must now be discarded once for all and the charge of provinces taken away from sun-dried bureaucrats of the type of Sir Michael O'Dwyer and Sir Reginald Craddock.

The bloodshed in the Punjab, which outdid all other Provinces in sending help during the war both in men and money, pointed to the administration or mal-administration of Sir Michael O'Dwyer as responsible for the nature and intensity of the outbreak. If ever there was a British ruler of India who deserved impeachment it is Sir Michael O'Dwyer. He was not only a tyrant and a snob of the worst order but he was incompetent also. One of the two things must have happened: Either he was out of touch with public feeling in the province or he deliberately provoked this disaster by a policy of strength. In either case he deserves to be publicly impeached and condemned for incompetence or brutality or possibly for both.

The following Summary of the orders passed by the officer commanding shows the nature of the martial law administered in the "most loyal" province in India, a province which has so far been considered to be the right arm of British Ráj in India.

I have italicised some words and sentences for special attention. The reader I hope will note the exceptions in favor of the Europeans and the Indian servants in the employ of the Europeans and also the reasonableness of the other orders, threatening punishment upon the owners of certain properties and requiring "all students," and all male persons belonging to private Colleges in Lahore to attend four times a day at a particular place for roll call. Order No. 14 is a gem of great brilliance.

I have omitted order No. 6 as unimportant. Orders from 8 to 12 inclusive are not available. What has been given above, however, is quite sufficient to show the nature of the martial law that has been applied to the Punjab, after five years of unquestioned and unrivalled loyalty to the British Empire, in the period of greatest danger that had overtaken it. Such is the reward of "loyalty."

No. 1

Whereas the Government of India has for good reasons proclaimed Martial Law in the districts of Lahore and Amritsar; and

Whereas superior military authority has appointed me to command troops and administer Martial Law in a portion of the Lahore district, . . . and whereas Martial Law may be briefly described as the will of the Military Commander in enforcing law, order and public safety:

I make known to all concerned that until further orders by me the following will be strictly carried out:

1. At 20·00 hours (8 o'clock) each evening a gun will be fired from the Fort, and from that signal till 05·00 hours (5 o'clock) on the following morning no person *other than a European* or a person in possession of a military permit signed by me or on my behalf will be permitted to leave his or her house or compound or the building in which he or she may be at 20 hours. During these prohibited hours no person other than those excepted above will be permitted to use the streets or roads, and any person found disobeying this order will be arrested, and if any attempt is made to evade or resist that person will be liable to be shot.

This and all other orders which from time to time I may deem necessary to make will be issued on my behalf from the water-works station in the city, whither every ward will keep at least four representatives from 6 A.M., till 17·00 hours (5 P.M.) daily to learn what orders, if any, are issued and to convey such orders to the inhabitants of their respective wards. *The onus of ascertaining the orders issued by me will rest on the people through their representatives.*

2. Loyal and law-abiding persons have nothing to fear from the exercise of Martial Law.

3. In order to protect the lives of his Majesty's soldiers and police under my command, I make known that if any firearm is discharged or bombs thrown at them the most drastic reprisals will instantly be made *against property surrounding the scene of the outrage.* Therefore it behooves all loyal inhabitants to see to it that no evil-disposed agitator is allowed on his premises.

4. During the period of Martial Law I prohibit all processions, meetings or other gatherings of more than 10 persons without my written authority, and any such meetings, gatherings or processions held in disobedience of this order will be broken up by force without warning.

5. I forbid any person to offer violence or cause obstruction to any person desirous of opening his shop or conducting his business or proceeding to his work or business. Any person contravening this order will be arrested, tried by a summary court and be liable to be shot.

6. At present the city of Lahore enjoys the advantage of electric lights and a water-supply; but the continuance of these supplies will depend on the good behaviour of the inhabitants and their prompt obedience to my orders.

No. 2

All tongas and tum-tums, (horse carriages) whether licensed for hire or otherwise, will be delivered up to the Military Officer appointed for that purpose at the Punjab Light Horse ground by 17·00 (5 P.M.) to-day — Tuesday, 15th April. Drivers will receive pay and horses be rationed.

No. 3

All motor-cars or vehicles of any descriptions will be delivered to the Military Officer appointed for that purpose at the Punjab club by 17·00 (5 P.M.) this day.

No. 4

By virtue of the powers vested in me I have prohibited the issue of third or intermediate class tickets at all railway stations in the Lahore Civil Command, *except only in the case of servants travelling with their European masters or servants or others in the employ of the Government.*

No. 5

Whereas, from information received by me, it would appear that shops, generally known as Langars, for the sale of cooked food, are used for the purpose of illegal meetings, and for the dissemination of seditious *propaganda*, and whereas I notice that all other shops (particularly in Lahore city) have been closed as part of an organized demonstration against his Majesty's Government, now, therefore, by virtue of the powers vested in me under Martial Law, I order that all such Langars or shops for the sale of cooked food in the Lahore civil area, except such as may be granted an exemption in writing by me shall close and cease to trade by 10·00 hours (10 A.M.) tomorrow, Wednesday, the 16th April, 1919.

Disobedience to this order will result in the confiscation of the contents of such shop and the arrest and trial by summary procedure of the owner or owners.

. . . .

No. 7

Whereas I have reason to believe that certain students of the D. A. V. College in Lahore are engaged in spreading seditious *propaganda* directed against his Majesty's Government, and whereas I deem it expedient in the interests of the preservation of law and order to restrict the activities of such students, I make the following order:—

All students of the said college now in this Command area will report themselves to the Officer Commanding Troops at the Bradlaugh Hall daily at the hours specified below and remain there until the roll of such students has been called by the principal or some other officer approved by me acting on his behalf, and until they have been dismissed by the Officer Commanding Troops at Bradlaugh Hall.

07·00 hours. (7 A.M.)
11·00 hours. (11 A.M.)
15·00 hours. (3 P.M.)
19·30 hours. (7.30 P.M.)

No. 8

Whereas some evilly-disposed persons have torn down or defaced notices and orders which I have caused to be exhibited for information and good government of the people in the Lahore (Civil) Command.

In future all orders that I have to issue under Martial Law *will be handed to such owners of property as I may select and it will be the duty of such owners of property to exhibit and keep exhibited and undamaged in the position on their property selected by me all such orders.*

The duty of protecting such orders will therefore devolve on the owners of property and failure to ensure the proper protection and continued exhibition of my orders will result in severe punishment.

Similarly, I hold responsible the owner of any property on which seditious or any other notices, proclamations or writing not authorized by me are exhibited.

. . . .

No. 13

Whereas information laid before me shows that a martial law notice issued by me and posted by my orders on a property known as the Sanatan Dharam College Hostel on Bahawalpur road, has been torn or otherwise defaced, in contravention of my Martial Law Notice No. 8.

Now, therefore, by virtue of the powers vested in me under martial law, I order the immediate arrest of *all male persons domiciled in the said hostel and their internment in the Lahore Fort* pending my further orders as to their trial or other disposal.

No. 14

Whereas practically every shop and business establishment in the area under my command has been closed in accordance with the *hartal* or organized closure of business directed against his Majesty's Government.

And whereas the continuance or resumption of such *hartal* is detrimental to the good order and governance of the said area.

And whereas I deem it expedient to cause the said *hartal* to entirely cease:

Now therefore by virtue of the powers vested in me by martial law I make the following order, namely:—

By 10·00 hours (10 A.M.) tomorrow (Friday), the 18th day of April, 1919, every shop and business establishment (except only *langare* referred to in martial law notice No. 5, dated 15th April, 1919) in the area under my command, shall open and carry on its business *and thereafter daily shall continue to keep open and carry on its business* during the usual hours up to 20·00 hours (8 P.M.) in exactly the same manner as before the creation of the said *hartal.*

And likewise I order that every skilled or other worker will from 10·30 hours (10.30 A.M.) tomorrow, resume and continue during the usual hours his ordinary trade, work or calling.

And I warn all concerned that if at 10·00 hours (10 A.M.) tomorrow, or at any subsequent time I find this order has been without good and valid reason disobeyed, the persons concerned will be arrested and tried under the summary procedure of martial law, and shops so closed will be opened and kept open by force, any resultant loss arising from such forcible opening will rest on the owners and on occupiers concerned.

And I further warn all concerned that this order must be strictly obeyed in spirit as well as in letter, that is to say, that to open a shop and then refuse to sell goods and to charge an exorbitant or prohibitive rate, will be deemed a contravention of this order.

[Note: Shops had evidently remained closed for seven days.]

No. 15

Whereas it has come to my knowledge that the present state of unrest is being added to and encouraged by the spreading of false, inaccurate or exaggerated reports or rumours:

Now, therefore, by virtue of the powers vested in me by martial law I give notice that *any person* found guilty of publishing, spreading or repeating, false, inaccurate or exaggerated reports in connection with the military or political situation, will be arrested and summarily dealt with under martial law.

No. 16

Whereas I have reason to believe that certain students of the Dyal Singh College in Lahore are engaged in spreading seditious propaganda directed against his Majesty's Government and whereas I deem it expedient in the interest of the preservation of law and order to restrict the activities of such students, I make the following order:—

All students of the said college now in this command area will report themselves to the officer commanding troops at the telegraph office daily at the hours specified below and remain there until the roll of such students has been called by the principal or some other officer approved by me acting on his behalf, and until they have been dismissed by the Officer Commanding Troops at the telegraph office:—

07·00 hours. (7 A.M.)
11·00 hours. (11 A.M.)
15·00 hours. (3 P.M.)
19·00 hours. (7 P.M.)

First parade at 11·00 hours (11 A.M.) on the (?) April, 1919.

"The latest order under martial law passed today makes it unlawful for more than two persons to walk abreast on any constructed or clearly defined pavement or side-walk in such area. Disobedience to this order will be punished by special powers under martial law. It shall also be illegal for any male person to carry or be found in possession of an instrument known as a *lathi*. All persons disobeying this order will be arrested and tried by summary proceedings under martial law."

. . . .

No. 24

Whereas I deem it expedient to make provision for the preservation of health and the greater comfort of British troops stationed in the area under my command,

And whereas a number of electric fans and lights are required in the buildings in which some of such troops are quartered,

Now therefore by virtue of the powers vested in me by martial law I authorize any officer appointed by me for that purpose to enter any college, public building, hostel, hotel, private or other residence or building and remove such number of electric lights and fans required for the purpose aforesaid,

And any attempt to obstruct such removal, or to hide, or to damage or to impair the immediate efficiency of any such fans or lights, will be summarily dealt with under martial law,

But nothing in this order shall authorize the removal of any fan or light from a room usually inhabited by a woman.

These are only a few of the orders we have been able to obtain.

For weeks the Punjab was in a state of terror. Almost all of the Native papers were either directly or indirectly suppressed or terrorized into silence. Numerous persons were arrested and placed for trial before military commissioners. Among them were a large number of the most honored men in the province. Legal counsel from ouside the province was denied to them, and admission of newspapermen into the province barred. In punishing the persons found guilty the military commissioners have awarded sentences, the parallel of which can only be found in the history of Czarism in Russia. Flogging in the public was resorted to in more than one place. In short, a complete reign of terror was established. So great was the terrorism that the whole country was thrown into such a paroxysm of rage, anger and despair as to make the people forget the desire for a political constitution at this terrible price.

Just as I am writing these lines I learn from the London *Times* that the reports of the two committees that were sent to India to inquire into (*a*) questions connected with the franchise and (*b*) the division of functions between the Government of India and local governments, and between the official and the popular elements in the local governments, have been published in Great Britain. In one of the Appendices is given a rather brief and inadequate summary of the recommendations of these committees published by the London *Times*. At this stage it is impossible to make any comments except that the franchise is by no means as broad as it could have been, the restriction of local residence on candidates for the provincial Legislative Councils extremely unreasonable, and the strength of the Provincial Councils very meagre. The recommendations are unsatisfactory in other respects also, specially the power granted to the Governor to dismiss ministers.

The question, however, is, "Will the Cabinet stand by these recommendations or will they allow them to be whittled down?" Mr. Montagu's bill, which is promised to be introduced in the House of Commons early in June, will answer the question.

In conclusion, I have to tender my thanks to my friend Dr. J. T. Sunderland for having read my proofs.

June 2, 1919.

LAJPAT RAI

CONTENTS

The Political Future of India

I

INTRODUCTORY

> Now we are faced with the greatest and the grimmest struggle of all. Liberty, Equality, Fraternity, not amongst men, but amongst nations — great and small, powerful and weak, exalted and humble, — equality, fraternity, amongst peoples as well as amongst men — that is the challenge which has been thrown to us. . . . My appeal to the people of this country, and, if my appeal can reach beyond it, is this, that we should continue to fight for the great goal of international right and international justice, so that never again shall brute force sit on the throne of justice, nor barbaric strength wield the sceptre of right.
>
> DAVID LLOYD GEORGE
>
> "Causes and Aims of the War." Speech delivered at Glasgow, on being presented with the freedom of that city, June 29, 1917

WE are told that the world is going to be reconstructed on entirely new lines; that all nations, big or small, shall be allowed the right of self-determination; that the weaker and backward peoples will no longer be permitted to be exploited and dominated by the stronger and the more advanced nations of the earth; and that justice will be done to all. "What we seek," says President Wilson, "is the reign of law, based upon the consent of the governed and sustained by the organized opinion of mankind."

The Indian people also form a part of the world that needs reconstructing. They constitute one-fifth of the human race, and inhabit about two million square miles of very fertile and productive territory. They have been a civilized people for thousands of years, though their civilization is a bit different from that of the West. We advisedly say "a bit different," because in fundamentals that civilization has the same basic origin as that of Greece and Rome, the three peoples having originally sprung from the same stock and their languages, also, being of common descent. For the last 150 years, or (even) more, India has been ruled by Great Britain. Her people have been denied any determining voice in the management of their own affairs. For over thirty years or more they have carried on an organized agitation for an autonomous form of Government within the British Empire. This movement received almost no response from the responsible statesmen of the Empire until late in the war. In the meantime some of the leaders grew sullen and downhearted, and, under the influence of bitter disappointment and almost of despair, took to revolutionary forms. The bulk of the people, however, have kept their balance and have never faltered in their faith in peaceful methods. When the war broke out the people of India at once realized the world significance of this titanic struggle and in no uncertain voice declared their allegiance to the cause of the Allies. Our masters, however, while gratefully accepting our economic contributions and utilizing the standing Indian army, spurned our offers for further military contributions. In the military development of the Indians they saw a menace to their supremacy in India.

The Russian Revolution first, and then the entry of the United States into the War, brought about a change in the point of view of the British statesmen. For the first time they realized that they could not win the war without the fullest coöperation of the people of India, both in the military and the economic sense and that the fullest coöperation of the United States also required as a condition precedent, quite a radical revision of their war aims. President Wilson's political idealism, his short, pithy and epigrammatic formulas compelled similar declarations by Allied statesmen. The British statesmen, at the helm of affairs, found it necessary to affirm their faith in President Wilson's principles and formulas if they would not let the morale of their own people at home suffer in comparison. In the meantime the situation in India was becoming uncomfortable. The Nationalists and the Home Rulers insisted on a clear and unequivocal declaration of policy on the lines of President Wilson's principles. The British statesmen in charge of Indian affairs, at Whitehall, were still temporizing when the report of the Royal Commission on the causes of the Mesopotamia disaster burst out on the half-dazed British mind like a bombshell. To the awakening caused by the report and its disclosures a material contribution was made by the outspoken, candid and clear-cut speech of a younger statesman, whose knowledge of the working of the Indian Government could not be questioned. When the Parliament, press and platform were all ablaze with indignation and shame at the supposed incompetence of the Indian Government, to whose inefficiency and culpable neglect of duty were ascribed the series of disasters that ended with the surrender of a British force at Kut-el-amara, Mr. Edwin Samuel Montagu, who had been an Under Secretary for India under Lord Morley and was at the time of the Mesopotamia disaster Minister of Munitions, came out with a strong and emphatic condemnation of the system and the form of Government under which the "myriads" of India lived and had their affairs managed. Mr. Montagu's opinion of the machinery of the Indian Government was expressed as follows:

"The machinery of Government in this country with its unwritten constitution, and the machinery of Government in our Dominions has proved itself sufficiently elastic, sufficiently capable of modification, to turn a peace-pursuing instrument into a war-making instrument. It is the Government of India alone which does not seem capable of transformation, and I regard that as based upon the fact that the machinery is statute-ridden machinery. The Government of India is too wooden, too iron, too inelastic, too antediluvian, to be any use for the modern purposes we have in view. I do not believe that anybody could ever support the Government of India from the point of view of modern requirements. But it would do. Nothing serious had happened since the Indian mutiny, the public was not interested in Indian affairs, and it required a crisis to direct attention to the fact that the Indian Government is an indefensible system of Government."

Regarding the Indian Budget Debates in Parliament, he said:

"Does anybody remember the Indian Budget Debates before the War? Upon that day the House was always empty. India did not matter, and the Debates were left to people on the one side whom their enemies sometimes called "bureaucrats," and on the other side to people whom their enemies sometimes called "seditionists," until it almost came to be disreputable to take part in Indian Debates. It required a crisis of this kind to realise how important Indian affairs were. After all, is the House of Commons to be blamed for that? What was the Indian Budget Debate? It was a purely academic discussion which had no effect whatever upon events in India, conducted after the events that were being discussed, had taken place."

He held that the salary of the Indian Secretary of State should be paid from the British Treasury, and then there would be real debates:

"How can you defend the fact that the Secretaries of State for India alone of all the occupants of the Front Bench, with the possible exception of the Chancellor of the Duchy of Lancaster, are not responsible to this House for their salaries, and do not come here with their Estimates in order that the House of Commons may express its opinion. . . .

"What I am saying now is in the light of these revelations of this inelasticity of Indian government. However much you could gloss over those indefensible proceedings in the past, the time has now come to alter them.

"The tone of those Debates is unreal, unsubstantial and ineffective. If Estimates for India, like Estimates for the Secretary of State for Foreign Affairs, and the Colonial Secretary were to be discussed on the floor of the House of Commons, the Debates on India would be as good as the Debates on foreign affairs. After all, what is the difference? Has it even been suggested to the people of Australia that they should pay the salary of the Secretary of State for the Colony? Why should the whole cost of that building in Charles Street, including the building itself, be an item of the Indian taxpayer's burden rather than of this House of Commons and the people of the country?"

Can and does the House of Commons control the India Office? Here is Mr. Montagu's answer.

"It has been sometimes questioned whether a democracy can rule an Empire. I say that in this instance the democracy has never had the opportunity of trying. But even if the House of Commons were to give orders to the Secretary of State, the Secretary of State is not his own master. In matters vitally affecting India, he can be overruled by a majority of his Council. I may be told that the cases are very rare in which the Council has differed from the Secretary of State for India. I know one case anyhow, where it was a very near thing, and where the action of the Council might without remedy have involved the Government of India in a policy out of harmony with the declared policy of the House of Commons and the Cabinet. And these gentlemen are appointed for seven years, and can only be controlled from the Houses of Parliament by a resolution carried in both Houses calling on them for their resignations. The whole system of the India Office is designed to prevent control by the House of Commons for fear that there might be too advanced a Secretary of State. I do not say that it is possible to govern India through the intervention of the Secretary of State with no expert advice, but what I do say is that in this epoch now after the Mesopotamia Report, he must get his expert advice in some other way than by this Council of men, great men though, no doubt, they always are, who come home after lengthy service in India to spend the first years of their retirement as members of the Council of India.

"Does any Member of this House know much about procedure in the India Office? I have been to the India Office and to other offices. I tell this House that the statutory organization of the India Office produces an apotheosis of circumlocution and red tape beyond the dreams of any ordinary citizen."

His own idea of what should be done at that juncture was thus expressed:

"But whatever be the object of your rule in India, the universal demand of those Indians whom I have met and corresponded with, is that you should state it. Having stated it, you should give some instalment to show that you are in real earnest, some beginning of the new plan which you intend to pursue, that gives you the opportunity of giving greater representative institutions in some form or other to the people of India. . . .

"But I am positive of this, that your great claim to continue the illogical system of Government by which we have governed India in the past is that it was efficient. It has been proved to be not efficient. It has been proved to be not sufficiently elastic to express the will of the Indian people; to make them into a warring Nation as they wanted to be. The history of this War shows that you can rely upon the loyalty of the Indian people to the British Empire — if you ever before doubted it! If you want to use that loyalty, you must take advantage of that love of country which is a religion in India, and you must give them that bigger opportunity of controlling their own destinies, not merely by Councils which cannot act, but by control, by growing control, of the Executive itself. Then in your next War — if we ever have War — in your next crisis, through times of peace, you will have a contented India, an India equipped to help. Believe me, Mr. Speaker, it is not a question of expediency, it is not a question of desirability. Unless you are prepared to remodel, in the light of modern experience, this century-old and cumberous machine, then, I believe, I verily believe, that you will lose your right to control the destinies of the Indian Empire."

The quick and resourceful mind of Premier Lloyd George at once grasped the situation. He lost no time in deciding what was needed. Probably over the head of his Tory colleagues, possibly with their consent, he gave the Indian portfolio to Mr. Montagu, and told him quietly to set to business. Mr. Montagu's first step was the announcement of August 20, 1917. On that date he made in the House of Commons the following memorable statement:

"The policy of His Majesty's Government, with which the Government of India are in complete accord, is that of the increasing association of Indians in every branch of the administration and the gradual development of self-governing institutions with a view to the progressive realisation of responsible government in India as an integral part of the British Empire. They have decided that substantial steps in this direction should be taken as soon as possible, and that it is of the highest importance as a preliminary to considering what these steps should be that there should be a free and informal exchange of opinion between those in authority at home and in India. His Majesty's Government have accordingly decided, with His Majesty's approval, that I should accept the Viceroy's invitation to proceed to India to discuss these matters with the Viceroy and the Government of India, to consider with the Viceroy the views of local Governments, and to receive with him the suggestions of representative bodies and others.

"I would add that progress in this policy can only be achieved by successive stages. The British Government and the Government of India, on whom the responsibility lies for the welfare and advancement of the Indian peoples, must be judges of the time and measure of each advance, and they must be guided by the co-operation received from those upon whom new opportunities of service will thus be conferred and by the extent to which it is found that confidence can be reposed in their sense of responsibility.

"Ample opportunity will be afforded for public discussion of the proposals which will be submitted in due course to Parliament."

It is obvious that the content of the second sentence of paragraph two in the above announcement is in fundamental opposition to the right of every nation to self-determination, a principle now admitted to be of general application (including, according to the British Premier, even the black races inhabiting the Colonies that were occupied by Germany before the War, within its purview). The people of India are not on the level of these races. Even if it be assumed that they are not yet in a position to exercise that right, fully and properly, it is neither right nor just to assume that they shall never be in that position even hereafter. The qualifications implied in that sentence are, besides, quite needless and superfluous. As long as India remains "an integral part of the British Empire" she cannot draft a constitution which does not meet with the approval of the British Parliament and the British Sovereign. It is to be regretted that the British statesmen could not rise equal to the spirit of the times and make an announcement free from that spirit of autocratic bluster and racial swagger which was entirely out of place at a time when they were making impassioned appeals to Indian manhood to share the burdens of Empire by contributing ungrudgingly in men and money for its defence. This attitude is somewhat inconsistent with the statements in paragraph 179 of the Montagu-Chelmsford Report, wherein, after referring to the natural evolution of "the desire for self-determination," the distinguished authors of the Report concede that "the demand that now meets us from the educated classes of India is no more than the right and natural outcome of the work of a hundred years."

In spite of this uncalled for reservation in the announcement, it is perfectly true that "the announcement marks the end of one epoch and the beginning of a new one." What makes the announcement "momentous," however, is not the language used, as even more high-sounding phrases have been used before by eminent British statesmen of the position of Warren Hastings, Macaulay, Munroe, Metcalf and others, but the fact that the statement has been made by the Secretary of State for India, as representing the Crown and the Cabinet who, in their turn, are the constitutional representatives of the people of Great Britain and Ireland. The statement is thus both morally and legally binding on the British people, though it will not acquire that character so far as the people of India are concerned, unless it is embodied in a Statute of Parliament. Is it too much to hope that when that stage comes the second sentence of the second paragraph might be omitted or so modified as to remove the inconsistency pointed out above?

We have no doubt, however, that the language of the announcement notwithstanding, the destiny of India remains ultimately in the hands of the Indians themselves. It will be determined, favorably or unfavorably, by the solidity of their public life, by the purity and idealism of the Indian public men to be hereafter entrusted with the task of administration, by the honesty and intensity of their endeavor to uplift the masses, both intellectually and economically, by the extent to which they reduce the religious and communal excuses that are being put forth as reasons for half-hearted advance, and by the amount of political unity they generate in the nation. The well known maxim that those who will must by themselves be free, is as good today as ever. They will have to do all this in order to persuade the British Parliament to declare them fit for responsible Government. Once they show their fitness by deeds and by actual conduct, no one can keep them in leading-strings.

Coming back to the announcement itself, would it not be well to bear in mind that what differentiates this announcement from the statutory declarations of the Act of 1833 and the Royal proclamation of 1858 is not the language used but the step or steps taken to ascertain Indian opinion, to understand and interpret it in accordance with the spirit of the times and the frankness and fairness with which the whole problem is stated in the joint report of the two statesmen, who are the present official heads of the Government of India. Nor can it be denied that the announcement and the report have received the cordial appreciation of the Indian leaders.

We, that is, the Indian Nationalists, have heretofore concerned ourselves more with criticism of the British administration than with the problem of construction, though our criticism has never been merely destructive. We have always ended with constructive suggestions. Henceforth, if the spirit of the announcement is translated into deeds it will be our duty to coöperate actively in constructive thought. Not that we refused coöperation in the past, but the conditions and the terms on which we were asked to coöperate made it impossible for us to make an effective response.

Several British critics of the Indian Nationalists have from time to time charged them with lack of constructive ability. They ignore the fact that political conditions in India were an effective bar to any display of ability.

The first attempt at constitution making was made by the Congress in 1915, and as such was bound to be rather timid and half-hearted. The situation since then has considerably improved and the discussions of the last twelve months have enabled the Secretary for India and the Viceroy to claim that, in certain respects, at least, their scheme is a more effective step towards responsible Government than the scheme promulgated jointly by the Congress and the Muslim League. How far that claim can be substantiated remains to be seen. This much is, however, clear: come what may, along with the rest of the world, India cannot go back to the pre-war conditions of life. The high functionaries of the British Government in India are also conscious of that fact, as one of them, the present Lieutenant Governor of the United Provinces of Agra and Oudh, a member of the Indian bureaucracy, remarked only recently in a speech at Allahabad:

"Nothing will ever be the same," said Sir Harcourt Butler; "this much is certain, that we shall have to shake up all our old ideals and begin afresh . . . we have crossed the watershed and are looking down on new plains. The old oracles are dumb. The old shibboleths are no more heard. Ideals, constitutions, rooted ideas are being shovelled away without argument or comment or memorial. . . . Our administrative machine belongs to another age. It is top-heavy. Its movements are cumbrous, slow, deliberate. It rejoices in delay. It grew up when time was not the object, when no one wanted change, when financial economy was the ruling passion of Governments, imperial and provincial. Now there are the stirrings of young national life, and economic springtime, a calling for despatch, quick response, bold experiment. Secretariats with enormous offices overhang the administration. An eminent ecclesiastic once told me that Rome had, by centuries of experience, reduced delay to a science; he used to think her mistress of postponement and procrastination, but the Government of India beat Rome every time. Only ecclesiatics could dare so to speak of the Government of India. I, for one, will not lay audacious hands on the chariot of the sun."

Coming, as it does, from a member of the Anglo-Indian bureaucracy, this statement means much more to the Indian people than even the words of the British Premier. If this statement is not mere camouflage, but represents a genuine change of heart on the part of the British bureaucracy in India, then it is all the more inexplicable to us why the new scheme of the Secretary for India and the Viceroy should breathe so much distrust of the educated classes of India. Any way, we have nothing but praise for the spirit of frankness and fairness which generally characterizes the report. However we might disagree with the conclusions arrived at, it is but right to acknowledge that the analysis of the problem and its constituting elements is quite masterly and the attempt to find a solution which will meet the needs of the situation *as understood by them* absolutely sincere and genuine. This fact makes it all the more necessary that Indian

Nationalists of all classes and all shades of opinion should give their best thought to the consideration of the problem in a spirit of construction and coöperation, as distinguished from mere fault-finding. Nor should it be forgotten for a moment that Mr. Montagu and Lord Chelmsford were all the time, when drawing their scheme, influenced by considerations of what, under the circumstances, is practicable and likely to be accepted, not only in India by the Anglo-Indian bureaucracy and the non-official European community, but by the *conservative* British opinion at home. It is the latter we have to convince and win over before the scheme has a ghost of a chance of being improved upon. When we say *conservative* opinion we include in that expression the Liberal and Labour Imperialists also. We should never forget that it is hard to part with power, however idealistic the individual vested with power may be, and it is still harder to throw away the chances of profit which one (and those in whom one is interested) have gained by efforts extending over a century and a half, and in the exercise of which one sees no immediate danger. I am of the opinion that hitherto Indian representation in England has been extremely meagre, spasmodic and inadequate to the needs of the situation. Outside England, India's voice has been altogether unheard. We have so far displayed an almost unpardonable simplicity in failing to recognise that the world is so situated these days that public opinion in one country sometimes reacts quite effectively on public opinion in another. It is our duty, therefore, to increase our representation in England and to keep our case before the world with fresh energy and renewed vigour, not in a spirit of carping denunciation of the British Government of India, but with a desire to educate and enlist liberal and right-minded opinion all over the world in our favor. In the following pages an attempt is made to examine the Montagu-Chelmsford report in a spirit of absolute candour and fairness, with practical suggestions for the improvement of the scheme in the light of Indian and British criticism thereupon.

II

DEMOCRACY IN INDIA

A nation that can sing about its defeat is a nation which is immortal.

DAVID LLOYD GEORGE

"Serbia." Speech delivered at the Serbian Lunch (Savoy Hotel), August 8, 1917.

BEFORE we take up the report of the Secretary for India and the Viceroy we intend to clear the ground by briefly meeting the almost universal impression that prevails in educated circles in the West, that democratic institutions are foreign to the genius of the Asiatic peoples and have never been known in India before. The latest statement to this effect was made by Mr. Reginald Coupland of the *Round Table Quarterly*, in an article he contributed to the *New Republic* (September 7, 1918) on "Responsible Government in India." We have neither the time nor the desire to go into the question as it relates to other Asiatic countries, though we might state, in general terms, that an impartial study of Asiatic history will disclose that in the centuries preceding the Reformation in Europe, Asia was as democratic or undemocratic as Europe. Since then democracy has developed on modern lines in Europe. While Asia has gradually disintegrated and fallen under foreign domination, Europe has progressed towards democracy. As regards India, however, we intend to refer briefly to what historical evidence is available.

Firstly, we wish to make clear what we understand by "democracy." There is no desire to enter into an academic discussion of the subject nor to burden this book with quotations from eminent thinkers and writers. In our judgment, the best definition of democracy so far has been furnished by Abraham Lincoln, viz., "the government of the people, by the people and for the people," regardless of the process or processes by which that government is constituted. One must, however, be clear minded as to what is meant by "the people." Does the expression include all the people that inhabit the particular territory to which the expression applies, regardless of sex, creed, color and race, or does it not? If it does, we are afraid there is little democracy even in Europe and America today. Until recently half of the population was denied all political power in the State by virtue of sex. Of the other half a substantial part was denied that right by virtue of economic status or, to be more accurate, by lack of economic status considered necessary for the exercise of political power. Even now the Southern States of the United States, Amendment XV to the American Constitution notwithstanding, effectively bar the colored people from the exercise of the franchise supposed to have been accorded to them by the amendment. In Europe, religious and social bars still exist in the constitutions of the different states. As Great Britain is supposed to be the most democratic country in Europe, we cannot do better than take the history of the growth of public franchise in that country as the best illustration of the growth of democracy in the terms of President Lincoln's formula.

Travelling backwards, the earliest democratic institutions known to Europe were those of Greece and Rome. In applying the term "democratic" to the city republics of Greece and Rome it is ignored that these "republics" were in no sense democratic. "Liberty," says Putnam Weale, "as it was understood in those two celebrated republics of Athens and Sparta meant abject slavery to the vast mass of the population, slavery every whit as cruel as any in the Southern States of the American Union before the war of Liberation. . . . In neither of these two republics did the freemen ever exceed twenty thousand, whilst the slaves ran into hundreds of thousands, and were used just as the slaves of Asiatics were used.[1] Thus the Greek republics were simply cities in which a certain portion of the inhabitants, little qualified to exercise them, had acquired exclusive privileges, while they kept the great body of their brethren in a state of abject slavery."[2] Discussing the nature of Roman citizenship Putnam Weale remarks (p. 25) that "in spite of the polite fiction of citizenship, the destinies of scores of millions were effectively disposed of by a few thousands." This was true not only with regard to the outlying parts of the Empire but even as to

[1] It is extremely doubtful if there were any slaves in India in the corresponding period of Indian history. At least, Megasthenes, the Greek ambassador at the Court of Chandra Gupta, did not find any in northern India, though his opinion is not accepted as quite correct. It is said that slavery did exist in a mild form in the southern peninsula.

[2] *The Conflict of Colour*, by PUTNAM WEALE, The Macmillan Co., New York, 1910, pp. 20–21.

Italy itself. "Roman liberty," continues Putnam Weale, "though an improvement on Greek conceptions, was like all liberty of antiquity confined really to those who, being present in the capital, could take an active part in the public deliberations. It was the liberty of city and not of a land. It was therefore exactly similar in practise, if not in theory, to the kind of liberty, which has always been understood in advanced Asiatic states — the system of Government by equipoise and nothing else. The idea of giving those who lived at a distance from the capital any means of representing themselves was never considered at all; and so, it was the populace of the capital (or only a part of it), aided by such force as might be introduced by the contesting generals or leaders, which held all the actual political power. *Representative Government* — the only effective guarantee of liberty of any sort — *had therefore not yet been dreamt of.*" [The italics are ours.]

Alison in his *History of Europe*, Vol. I, says: "The states of Florence, Genoa, Venice and Pisa were not in reality free; they were communities *in which a few individuals had usurped* the rights, and disposed of the fortunes, of the great bulk *of their fellow citizens, whom they governed as subjects or indeed as slaves.* During the most flourishing period of their history, the citizens of all Italian republics did not amount to 20,000, and these privileged classes held as many million in subjection. The citizens of Venice were 2500 and those of Genoa 4500, those of Pisa, Siena, Lucea and Florence taken together, not above 6000." [Italics ours.] Coming to more modern times we find it stated by Morse Stephens in his *History of Revolu-*

tionary Europe that "the period which preceded the French Revolution and the era of war from the troubles of which Modern Europe was to be born may be characterised as that of the benevolent despots. The State was everything, the nation nothing." Speaking of the eighteenth-century conditions in Europe, Stephens remarks that "the great majority of the peasants of Europe were throughout that century absolute serfs"; also that "the mass of the population of Central and Eastern Europe was purely agricultural and in its poverty expected naught but the bare necessaries of existence. The cities and consequently the middle classes formed but an insignificant factor in the population." These quotations reveal the real character of the European democracy in ancient and mediæval and even in early modern Europe up to the end of the eighteenth century, or, to be more accurate, to the time of the French Revolution. Compare this with the following facts about the political institutions of India, during the ancient and mediæval times:

(1) First we have the testimony of ancient Brahmanic and Buddhistic literature, preserved in their sacred books, about the right of the people to elect their rulers; the duty of the rulers to obey *the law* and their obligation to consult their ministers as well as the representatives of the public in all important affairs of State.

The Vedic literature contains references to non-monarchial forms of Government,[3] makes mention of elected rulers and of assemblies of people, though the normal as distinguished from universal form of Govern-

[3] *Public Administration in Ancient India*, by P. BANERJEA, Macmillan, London, 1916, p. 42.

ment according to Professor Macdonald was by Kings, "a situation which, as in the case of the Aryan invaders of Greece and of the German invaders of England, resulted almost necessarily in strengthening the monarchic element of the constitution." [4]

In the *Aitreya Brahmana* occur terms which are translated by some as representing the existence of "self-governed" and "kingless" states. These authorities have been collected, translated and explained by K. P. Jayas Wal and Narendranath Law in a series of articles published in the *Modern Review* of Calcutta.

The *Mahabharata*, the great Hindu epic, makes mention of kingless states or oligarchies. "In fact," says Mr. Banerjea, "all the Indian nations of these times possessed popular institutions of some type or other." [5]

Professor Rhys Davids has said, in his *Buddhist India*, that "the earliest Buddhist records reveal the survival side by side with more or less powerful monarchies, of republics with either complete or modified independence." He names ten such republics in Northern India alone. In regard to the system of Government effective within one of the tribes that constituted a republic of their own, the same scholar observes: "The administrative and judicial business of the clan was carried out in public assembly, at which young and old were alike present in their common Mote Hall. A single chief — how and for what period chosen we do not know — was elected an officeholder, presiding over the sessions, or, if there were no sessions, over the State. He bore the title of *Raja*,

[4] *Vedic India*, by Macdonnell & Keith. Vol. II. p. 210.

[5] Banerjea, p. 43.

which must have meant something like the Roman Consul or the Greek Archon." [6] There is no evidence of the existence of slaves or serfs in these communities. Evidently all were freemen.

(2) We have the evidence of Greek historians of the period who accompanied Alexander in his Asiatic Campaign, or who, after Alexander's death, represented Greek monarchs at the courts of Indian rulers. "Even as late as the date of Alexander's invasion," says Mr. Banerjea, "many of the nations of the Punjab lived under democratic institutions." Speaking of one of them called Ambasthas (Sambastai), the Greek author of *Ancient India* says: "They lived in cities in which the democratic form of Government prevailed." "Curtius," adds Mr. Banerjea, "mentions a powerful Indian tribe, where the form of Government was democratic, and not regal." [7] Similarly Arrian, another Greek writer, is quoted as mentioning several other independent, self-governing tribal communities who lived under democratic forms of government and bravely resisted the advance of Alexander. One of them, when making submission to Alexander, told him that "they were attached more than any others to freedom and autonomy, and that their freedom they had preserved intact from the time Dionysos came to India until Alexander's invasion." [8] There were some others which had an aristocratic form of Government. In one of them mentioned in *Ancient*

[6] *Buddhist India*. p. 9.

[7] *Ancient India, Alexander's Invasion* (McCrindle, p. 292), quoted by Mr. Banerjea. p. 44.

[8] Arrian, *Anabasis* (McCrindle), p. 154; quoted by Mr. Banerjea, p. 154. If the Greek writers were familiar with the conceptions of democracy and republicanism they knew what they meant by the use of these terms in relation to Indian institutions.

India, "the administration was in the hands of three hundred wise men."

Another Greek writer, Diodoros, speaks of *Patala* as "a City of great note with a political constitution drawn on the same lines as the Spartan." It may safely be presumed that the Greek meant what he said. Chanakya, the author of a great treatise on political science, mentions many powerful oligarchies that existed down to the fourth century A. D. In one of the inscriptions, said to be of the sixth century A. D., the *Malavas* are referred to as living under a republican form of Government.[9]

(3) Even when kingship became an established institution the idea that the King was only a servant of the people survived for a long time. His "remuneration" was fixed at one-sixth of the produce. His subjects had the right to depose him or to turn him out if he failed in his duty. The authorities on these points are collected by Mr. Banerjea on pp. 72 and 73 of his book.

(4) Similarly many authorities are quoted by Mr. Banerjea on pp. 74 and 75 of his learned work showing that, according to Hindu ideals practised in ancient times, the king was not above the law. He was not an autocrat. He was as much bound by the law as his subjects. Laws were not made by kings. "Legislation was not among the powers entrusted to a king," says Mr. Banerjea. "There is no reference in early Vedic literature to the exercise of legislative authority by the king, though later it is an essential part of his duties," says Prof. Macdonell.[10]

[9] BANERJEA. p. 46.
[10] MACDONELL & KEITH, *Vedic Index*, Vol. II, p. 214.

(5) Assemblies and councils are quite frequently mentioned both in the Rig and the Atharva Vedas. "The popular assembly was a regular institution in the early years of the Buddhistic age (500 to 300 B.C.)" Chanakya mentions that in the King's Council the decision of the majority should prevail.[11] Sukraniti lays down elaborate rules of procedure for the conduct of business in these assemblies. "The Council was the chief administrative authority in the kingdom. The King was supposed not to do anything without the consent of the Council."[12] In *Kerala* State, South India, during the first and second centuries of the Christian Era, there were five assemblies one of which consisted of "representatives of the people summoned from various parts of the State."[13] "From the Ceylon inscriptions we learn that in that island all measures were enacted by the King in Council, and all orders were issued by and under the authority of the Council."

While all this is true of Ancient India, we cannot claim the existence of the same system of Government for mediæval India. Even as regards Ancient India, all that is claimed is that it possessed as much democracy, if not more, as Ancient Greece or Ancient Rome. The non-existence of slavery in Northern India gives it therefore a superior character to that of the Ancient republics of Greece and Rome. In the South, it is believed slavery did exist. Coming to mediaeval times generally known as the Mohammedan period of Indian History consisting of two epochs, from 400 to 1200 A.D. and from 1200 to 1800 A.D.,

[11] BANERJEA. p. 95.

[12] Footnote, *Ibid.*, p. 96. Original authority quoted by Mr. BANERJEA in footnote on p. 103.

[13] *Ibid.*, p. 104.

we notice that the country enjoyed a durable kind of government, cities under absolute rule, and villages, as before, self-governed. The absolute rule was a benevolent or malevolent despotism according to the character of the Hindu or Moslem sovereign who reigned. But in the villages India maintained a democratic form of government right up to the beginning of British rule; and though under British rule, it has been practically superseded by the rule of the officials, yet in some parts of the country the spirit is still alive, as will appear from the following testimony recorded by Mr. Sidney Webb in his Preface to Mr. John Matthai's volume, *Village Government in British India:*

"One able collector of long service in Central India informed me that he had been, until a few months before, totally unaware that anything of the sort existed in any of the villages over which he ruled. But being led to make specific inquiries on the subject, he had just discovered, in *village after village, a distinctly effective if somewhat shadowy, local organization, in one or other form of panchayat, which was, in fact, now and then giving decisions on matters of communal concern, adjudicating civil disputes, and even condemning offenders to reparation and fine.* Such a Local Government organization is, of course, 'extra-legal,' and has no statutory warrant, and, in the eyes of the British tribunals, possesses no authority whatever. But it has gone on silently existing, possibly for longer than the British Empire itself, and is still effectively functioning, merely by common consent and with the very real sanction of the local public opinion."

Mr. Matthai has also made a similar remark in Paragraph 22 of his book (Introductory).

Village councils ordinarily called village *panchayats*

have often been confounded with caste panchayats and that fact has been emphasised to prove that these Indian *panchayats* were or are anything but democratic. Mr. Sidney Webb and Mr. John Matthai both have controverted that position and upon good evidence. Says Mr. Webb:

"One suggestion that these fragments of indigenous Indian Local Government seem to afford is that we sometimes tend to exaggerate the extent to which the cleavages of caste have prevailed over the community of neighbourhood. How often is one informed, 'with authority,' that the *panchayat* of which we catch glimpses must be only a caste *panchayat!* It is plain, on the evidence, that however frequent and potent may be the *panchayat* of a caste, there have been and still are *panchayats* of men of different castes, exercising the functions of a Village Council over villagers of different castes. How widely prevalent these may be not even the Government of India can yet inform us. But if people would only look for traces of Village Government, instead of mainly for evidences of caste dominance, we might learn more on the subject."

Later on in the same paragraph Mr. Webb remarks that, even where caste exists it has, in fact, permitted a great deal of common life, and that it is compatible with active village councils.

Besides the evidence furnished by the texts of Hindu codes, law books and political treatises (like the *Arthasastra* of *Kautalaya*), and Nítí Shástrá, etc., other good evidence has been produced by Mr. Matthai in support of the above-mentioned proposition.

In Paragraph 23 he refers to the *Madras Epigraphic Report*, 1912–13, in support of the statement that "there were village assemblies in South India in the tenth century A.D., which 'appear to have consisted of all the residents of a village including cultivators, professionals and merchants.'"

"In the *Private Diary of Anandaranga Pillay*, who served as agent to Dupleix, the French Governor in South India in the middle of the eighteenth century, there is an entry referring to a village meeting to consider a case of desecrating the village temple 'in which people of all castes — from the Brahman to the Pariah — took part.'"

In Paragraph 24, he points out that a village council (*Panchayat*) might either be an assembly of all the inhabitants of the village or only a select committee consisting of representatives selected on some recognized principle. The first are common among less developed communities like those of the aboriginal tribes and the latter in more highly organized communities.

Evidences of bigger assemblies consisting of representatives of more than one village, sometimes of more than one district, to decide cases of importance or dispute between whole villages are also cited in Paragraphs 26 and 27 and 32. On the strength of certain South Indian Inscriptions relating to the Tamil Kingdoms of the 10th century A.D., it is stated that the administration of the village was carried on by no less than five or six committees, each vested with jurisdiction relating to certain definite departments of village life, though there was no fixed rule on the point. In Paragraphs 33 and 34 the mode of election to the committees and the qualifications for membership are set down in detail. The procedure seems to have been quite elaborate, though suited to the level of intelligence of the people concerned. These village councils and committees looked after education, sanitation, poor relief, public works, watch and ward, and the administration of justice. To describe the methods by which these departments of village life were administered by the village councils requires too much space, but we give two excerpts from Chapter II on education:

"The history of village education in India goes back perhaps to the beginnings of the village community. The schoolmaster had a definite place assigned to him in the village economy, in the same manner as the headman, the accountant, the watchman, and the artisans. He was an officer of the village community, paid either by rent-free lands or by assignments of grain out of the village harvest."

"The outstanding characteristics of the schools of the Hindu village community were: (1) that they were democratic, and (2) that they were more secular than spiritual in their instruction and their general character. . . . Nevertheless, when we speak of the democratic character of these early Hindu schools, it is to be understood that they were democratic only in this sense, that they were open not merely to the priestly caste but to all the four superior castes alike. There was never any question of admitting into the schools those who lay outside the regular caste system whose touch would have meant pollution, nor to the great aboriginal populations of the country."

"This is very similar to the public schools in the Southern States, in the United States, where schools for the white children are closed to coloured children and vice versa."

From what has been stated above it appears that the general impression that democratic institutions are *entirely* foreign to India is nothing but the survival of a prejudice originally due to ignorance of Indian history. In collecting his evidence Mr. Matthai has principally drawn upon South Indian sources. There can be no doubt that abundant evidence of a similar kind is available as regards North India and is waiting to be collected, collated and sifted by other Matthais. We do not contend that India had the same kind of representative institutions as Modern Europe has. In fact no part of the world had. They are all recent developments. The democratic nature of an institution does not depend on the methods of election but on the people's right to express their will, directly, or through their representatives, in the management of their public affairs. It is clear that that idea was never altogether absent from Indian life either in theory or in practise. Even under the most absolute autocracies, the bulk of the people managed their collective affairs themselves. They organised and maintained schools; arranged and paid for sanitation; built public works; provided for watch and ward; administered justice, and for all these purposes raised revenues and spent them in a democratic way. They did so, not only as regards the internal affairs of a village, but applied the same principles in the larger life of their district or districts. Such a people cannot be said to have *always* lived a life dictated and held together by force. Nor can it be said with justice that the introduction of modern democratic methods in such a country, among such a people, would be the introduction of an exotic plant, with the spirit and working of which it will take them centuries to be familiar.

III

THE PRESENT IDEALS

> The wishes, the desires, and the interests of the people of these countries [speaking of German colonies] themselves must be the dominant factor in settling their future government.
>
> DAVID LLOYD GEORGE
>
> "Causes and Aims of the War." Speech delivered at Glasgow, on being presented with the freedom of that city, June 29, 1917.

EVERY nation has a fundamental right to determine, fix and work out her own ideals. Any interference with this right by individuals or nations of foreign origin is unnatural and unjust. The consent of the governed is the only logical and just basis of governments. These principles have been reiterated with added force and masterly eloquence by President Wilson in his addresses during the War. They have been accepted and adopted by the Allied statesmen. No statesman or publicist of standing in any of the Allied countries can dare question the principles. The difficulty, however, arises when we come to apply them practically. At this point the practical politician's genius for diplomacy discovers flaws that provide excuses for the non-application of those principles if such course seems helpful to his nation or his sovereign.

President Wilson has asseverated that "the day of conquest and aggrandisement is gone," which, in plain language, means that the day of Imperialism is over. And, in conformity with the principle stated in the Declaration of Independence, that "All nations have the right to assume among the powers of the earth the separate and equal station to which the laws of nature and nature's God entitle them," President Wilson has also said that "every people have a right to choose the sovereignty under which they shall live"; that "national aspirations must be respected, and that 'self determination' is not a mere phrase; it is an imperative principle of action, which statesmen will henceforth ignore at their peril." Yet as *practical men* we must not ignore the facts of life. The world is not at once going to be an ideal place to live in even if it may become one. It may be that the advanced nations of the earth which just now divide the political and economic control of the world between themselves may accept the underlying policy of the following statement (of President Wilson) that

"This war had its roots in the disregard of the rights of small nations and of nationalities which lacked the union and the force to make good their claim to determine their own allegiance and their own forms of political life."

and the proposed League of Nations might see that a continuance of the injustice thus far done to small or backward nations is no longer permitted. Being practical men, however, we cannot build on the assumption that at the end of this war the world is at once to be transformed into a paradise and that full justice will be done to all nations and all peoples alike. We already notice a tendency to restrict the application and the enforcement of these principles to the nations of Europe by the more frequent use of the term "free nations." "Free nations" do not need to be freed. It will be wise, therefore not to be carried off our feet by these declarations and statements. Mr. Montagu and Lord Chelmsford have pointedly reminded us of the Indian saying, "hanoz Delhi Dúr Ast" (i.e. "Delhi is yet far away"). But even if they had not done so we were not so simple as to be swept away by the mere language of the war declarations. The wording of the announcement of August 20, 1917, itself did not leave us in doubt about the truth of the saying quoted by Mr. Montagu and Lord Chelmsford. We have, therefore, to test our ideals and aspirations by the touchstone of practicability and expediency. Happily for us there is, in theory, at least, a full agreement between the political goal set up by the Indian Nationalists of the Congress school (since endorsed by the Home Rulers) and that set up by the authors of the announcement of August 20th. This goal is "Self-Government within the Empire on terms of equality with the other parts of it," in the language of the Congress school or, "Responsible Government as an integral part of the British Empire," in the language of the announcement. There is a party of Indian politicians who want complete independence, but at present their number is so limited that we need not take serious consideration of their position in the matter. The vast bulk of the educated classes are agreed:

(*a*) That they are content to remain within the British Empire if they are allowed a status of equality with the self-governing dominions of the Empire.

(*b*) That what they want is an autonomous Government on the lines of Canada, Australia and the South African Union.

(*c*) That they do not want any affiliation with any other Foreign Government.

Much has been written and said about the loyalty of the people of India to the British Government. Opinions, however, differ as to its nature. Some say it is the loyalty of a helpless people or, in other words, a loyalty dictated by fear or force. Others say it is the loyalty of opportunism. The British maintain that the loyalty is the outcome of a genuine and sincere appreciation of the blessings of the British Empire. Be that as it may, it is in the interest of both to bring about circumstances and conditions which would transform this loyalty whatever its nature into one of genuine affection and interest. The announcement of August 20, 1917, may be considered as a first step towards the creation of such loyalty, but much will depend on the steps that are taken to give practical effect to the policy embodied in the said announcement and on the spirit in which the proposed reforms are carried out. Mr. Montagu and Lord Chelmsford's conception of the "eventual future of India is a sisterhood of states, self-governing in all matters of purely local or provincial interest, in some cases corresponding to existing provinces, in others perhaps modified in area according to the character and economic interests of their people. Over this congeries of States should preside a Central Government increasingly representative of and responsible to the people of all of them; dealing with matters, both internal and external, of common interest to the whole of India; acting as arbiter in interstate relations and representing the interests of all India on equal terms with the self-governing units of the British Empire."[1] The only changes that we would propose in the language of this statement are (i) the omission of the word "increasingly" which is rather misplaced in the conception of an ideal, and (ii) the substitution of the word "Commonwealth" in place of "Empire." His Highness the Aga Khan considers the use of the term "responsible" government instead of "self-government" in the announcement as unfortunate because it carries the technical meaning of a government responsible for its existence to an assembly elected by the people. On the other hand, self-government can comprise many and varied forms of expression of the popular will. Further, he is convinced that the words "responsible government" were used in order to carry with the Secretary of State and the Prime Minister some more conservative members of the small war cabinet. It was camouflaged so that the Executive government hereafter might contain Englishmen, while at the same time the administration became sufficiently liberal to be responsible to the people. With due respect to the Aga Khan we do not see the logical connection between the two. Responsible government may or may not involve the necessary inclusion of Englishmen in the Cabinet. Although we may not approve of the interpretation of the

[1] Paragraph 349 of the *Report*.

expression "responsible" government given to it by the authors of the report, in our judgment its use as an ideal to be attained expresses more forcibly the right of the people to choose their government than the use of the general term "self government" would.

IV

THE STAGES

> There is no protection for life, property, or money in a State where the criminal is more powerful than the law. The law of nations is no exception, and, until it has been vindicated, the peace of the world will always be at the mercy of any nation whose professors have assiduously taught it to believe that no crime is wrong so long as it leads to the aggrandisement and enrichment of the country to which they owe allegiance.
>
> DAVID LLOYD GEORGE
>
> "No Halfway House." Speech delivered at Gray's Inn, December 14, 1917.

IN the chapter on ideals we have shown that there is almost complete agreement between the bulk of Indian educated men and the British authorities as to the immediate goal of Government in India. There is no such agreement, however, as regards the stages by which that goal is to be reached, nor on the steps which should be immediately taken to carry us to the first stage. The four formulas by which Mr. Montagu and Lord Chelmsford profess to be guided in their recommendations are not accepted in their entirety by the spokesmen of the Indian people. These formulas are:

(1) There should be as far as possible complete popular control in local bodies and the largest possible independence for them of outside control. (Paragraph 188.)

(2) The provinces are the domain in which the earlier steps towards the progressive realization of responsible government should be taken. Some measure of responsibility should be given at once, and our aim is to give complete responsibility as soon as conditions permit. This involves at once giving the provinces the largest measure of independence, legislative, administrative, and financial, of the Government of India which is compatible with the due discharge by the latter of its own responsibilities. (Paragraph 189.)

(3) The Government of India must remain wholly responsible to Parliament, and saving such responsibility, its authority in essential matters must remain indisputable pending experience of the effect of the changes now to be introduced in the provinces. In the meantime the Indian Legislative Council should be enlarged and made more representative and its opportunities of influencing government increased. (Paragraph 190.)

(4) In proportion as the foregoing changes take effect, the control of Parliament and the Secretary of State over the Government of India and provincial Governments must be relaxed. (Paragraph 191.)

There is no difficulty in accepting the first and the fourth formulas. There is some complaint that the actual steps recommended for immediate adoption to give effect to the policy of the first formula are not in keeping with the spirit of the formula and are inadequate. But this we can reserve for future consideration.

No objection can be taken to the first and the last sentences of the second formula; though there is a great divergence of opinion as regards the content of the second. It is maintained by some, and their number is by no means small,[1] that full responsibility should be conceded to the provinces at once and that there is nothing in the conditions mentioned in the report which justifies the postponement thereof.

The third formula, however, is the one about which there is not even a semblance of agreement. All political parties and all qualified persons in India (we mean, of course, Indians of Indian origin) are agreed that the assumptions and presumptions upon which this formula is based are wrong and unacceptable. Native Indian opinion is fairly unanimous on the point.

There are some who claim full autonomy at once. There are others who claim full autonomy except as regards foreign relations, the control of native States, the Army and the Navy. All insist that a beginning of responsible Government must be made in the Central Government also, and point out the absolute necessity of conceding some measure, even if not full, of fiscal autonomy. They can see no reason why "the Government of India must remain wholly responsible to Parliament" and why "its authority must remain indisputable." On these matters Indian opinion joins issue with the distinguished authors of the report. We will revert to the subject in another chapter.

1. The non-official members of Bengal, Bombay and the United Provinces have made that demand, which has been endorsed by the Indian National Congress and the All-Indian Muslim League.

V

THE CONDITIONS OF THE PROBLEM

> Let us, at any rate, make victory so complete that national liberty, whether for great nations or for small nations, can never be challenged. That is the ordinary law. The small man, the poor man, has the same protection as the powerful man. So the little nation must be as well guarded and protected as the big nation.
>
> DAVID LLOYD GEORGE
>
> "The Pan-German Dream." Speech delivered at Queen's Hall on the third anniversary of the Declaration of War, August 4, 1917.

THE eminent authors of the report have devoted an entire chapter to a consideration of what they call the "conditions of the problem." These may be considered under two different heads: (a) those that necessitate a rather radical reorganisation of the Government of India; (b) those that prevent the authors from recommending immediate responsible government and justify the limitations of their scheme.

IMMENSITY OF THE PROBLEM AND THE GRAVITY OF THE TASK

Before we take up the two sets of facts relied upon by them in support of either position we may express our general agreement with them as regards the gravity of the task and the immensity of the problem. The size of the country and the vastness of its population are the measure of the extent of the problem. The existence of powerful vested interests at present possessed by the ruling race which may be interfered with by extended changes in the system of Government are the measure of its gravity. "The welfare and happiness of hundreds of millions of people," which the authors say are in issue cannot be adequately provided for by any autocratic system of Government however benevolent its purpose, and however magnificent its organisation. An "absolute government" is an anachronism, but when it is foreign it is doubly so. To bring out "the best in the people" for their own "welfare and happiness" as well as for that of mankind in general, it is necessary that the people should be free to develop on their own lines, manage their own affairs, evolve their own life, subject only to such restrictions as the general interests of humanity demand; and subject to such guidance as the better placed and more experienced people of the earth can furnish.

The people of India are willing to be guided in their development towards modern democracy by the people of Great Britain and they would be grateful for their coöperation in this difficult task, but they must be made to realize that the task is their own and that they should undertake it in a spirit of courageous faith — faith in their destiny, faith in their ability to achieve it, and faith in the friendship of the great British nation. The test of all measures in relation to the Government of India in future should be, not how far the people of India can coöperate, how far they can be entrusted with responsibility, but how far it is necessary *in their interests* to control and check them. The difference between the two points of view is fundamental and important. Mr. Montagu and Lord Chelmsford have looked at the problem from the former point of view; the Indian leaders want them to look at it from the latter. They want the great British nation to recognise the justice of India's claim to manage her own affairs, and to keep in their hands in future only such control as is absolutely necessary (a) to enable the Indian people to conduct their business efficiently and successfully, (b) to make them fulfill their obligations to the great Commonwealth of nations of which they hope soon to be a component part. As long as British statesmen insist on looking at the problem from the former point of view, they will make mistakes and raise a not entirely unreasonable suspicion of their motives. The moment they adopt the other point of view, they remove all grounds of distrust and create an atmosphere of friendliness in which they can deal with the problem in a spirit of mutual trust, absolute frankness and candid perspicacity. There are many contentions of the British statesmen which the educated Indians would gladly admit to be valid and necessary were they sure that their admission would not be used against them by the power whom they habitually regard as their adversary. There is much in this report which could at once be struck out if both parties were actuated by feelings of mutual trust and friendliness. It cannot be denied that many of the proposed restrictions on the power of the popular assemblies and the would-be

Indian Administrators are the outcome of distrust. It is no wonder then that the Indian leaders in their turn are not quite sure of the face value of the many professions of good will that characterise the scheme. It is for the removal of this distrust that we appeal as earnestly as we can to the better mind of Great Britain.

In looking at the conditions of the problem, there is another fallacy which underlies the oft-exaggerated estimates of the blessings of British rule in India by British statesmen and British publicists. They compare the India of today with the India of 1757 and at once jump to the conclusion that "the moral and material civilisation of the Indian people has made more progress in the last fifty years than during all the preceding centuries of their history." The proper comparison is of the Great Britain, the France, the United States, the Germany, the Italy and the Japan of 1757, with the India of that year and of India's progress within the last century and a half, or even within the last 50 years, with the progress of these countries in the same period. We have no desire to withhold credit for what Great Britain has done in India, but what she has misdone or could have done but failed to do, by virtue of her rule in India being absolute and thus necessarily conditioned by limitations inevitable in a system of absolute rule, should not be forgotten.

The Indian critics of British rule in India have repeatedly pointed out that what they condemned and criticised was the *system* and not the personnel of the Government, and the distinguished authors of the Report "very frankly recognise that the character of political institutions reacts upon the character of the people" and that the exercise of responsibilities calls forth capacity for it (Paragraph 130), which mainly accounts for the conditions that serve as reasons for withholding responsible government from the Indian people. In discussing "the basis of responsibility" Mr. Montagu and Lord Chelmsford very properly point out that the qualities necessary for it are only developed by exercise and that though "they are greatly affected by education, occupation and social organisation" "they ultimately rest on the traditions and habits of the people." "We cannot go simply to statistics for the measure of these things." Yet, unfortunately, it is exactly these statistics that seem to have influenced them largely in the framing of their half-hearted measures. The two dominating conditions which obsess them are (1) that the immense masses of the people are poor, ignorant and helpless far beyond the standards of Europe; and (2) that there runs through Indian society a series of cleavages — of religion, race and caste — which constantly threaten its solidarity.

We admit the existence of these conditions, but we do not admit that they are an effective bar to the beginnings of responsible government even on that scale on which European countries had it when the conditions of life in those countries were no better than they are now in India.

It is said that 226 of 244 millions of people in British India live a rural life: "agriculture is the one great occupation of the people" and "the proportion of these who even give a thought to matters beyond the horizon of their villages is very small." We ask did not similar conditions exist in Great Britain, France and Germany before the inauguration of the Industrial Revolution, and if they did, did they stand in the way of their people getting responsible government or parliamentary institutions? Everyone knows what the conditions in France were in years immediately preceding the Revolution. Italy was no better off in the middle of the nineteenth century. Perhaps it is not much better even today. The masses of the people in these and other countries of Europe, including Great Britain, were far more ignorant, poor and helpless when these countries obtained parliamentary government than they are in India today. And the authors of the report are not unaware that similar concerns are perhaps the main interests of the population of some country districts in the United Kingdom even today. In several of the Balkan States, Roumania, Serbia and Bulgaria — in Italy and in the component parts of Russia — the conditions are no better, yet their right to autonomous government, nay, even to absolute independence, is hardly questioned. Moreover, as has been pointed out by Mr. Sidney Webb,

"It is a mistake to assume that a land of villages necessarily means what is usually implied by the phrase, a people of villagers. In truth, India, for all its villages, has been also, at all known periods, and to-day still is, perhaps, to a greater extent than ever before, what Anglo-Saxon England, for instance was *not* or the South African Republic in the days before gold had been discovered, and what the Balkan peninsula even at the present time may perhaps not be, namely a land of flourishing cities, of a distinctly urban civilization, exhibiting not only splendid architecture, and the high development of the manufacturing arts made possible by the concentration of population and wealth, but likewise — what is much more important — a secretion of thought, an accumulation of knowledge, and a development of literature and philosophy which are not in the least like the characteristic products of villages as we know them in Europe or America. And to-day, although the teeming crowds who throng the narrow lanes of Calcutta or Benares, Bombay or Poona, Madras or Hyderabad, or even the millions who temporarily swarm at Hardwar or Allahabad or Puri may include only a small percentage of the whole population, yet the Indian social order does not seem to be, in the European understanding of the phrase, either on its good or on its bad side, essentially one of the villagers. The distinction may be of importance, because the Local Government developed by peoples of villages, as we know of them in Anglo-Saxon England, in the early days of the South African Republic, and in the Balkan States, is of a very different type from that which takes root and develops, even in the villages, in those nations which have also a City life, centers of religious activity, colleges and universities, and other 'nodal points,' from which emanate, through popular literature, pilgrimages, and the newspaper press, slow but far-spreading waves of thought and feeling, and aspirations which it is fatal to ignore." [1]

We have also quoted, in the chapter on "Democracy in India," the statement of Morse Stephens, about the condition of the people of Europe in the eighteenth century.

EDUCATIONAL BACKWARDNESS

"The Educational returns," remark the authors of the Report, "tell us much the same story," viz., the

[1] *Village Government in British India*, by JOHN MATTHAI. Preface by SIDNEY WEBB, p. xv.

appalling dissimilarity of conditions in Europe and in India. While it is painfully true that the percentage of illiteracy in India is greater than in any of the countries of Europe, we cannot admit that that fact is a fatal bar to the beginnings of responsible government in India or to the granting of a democratic constitution to the country. Literacy is, no doubt, a convenient, but by no means a sure index of the intelligence of the people, even much less of their character. The political status of a country is determined more by intelligence and character than by literacy. In these the people of India are inferior to none. By that we do not mean that they are possessed of the same kind of political responsibility as the people of the United Kingdom or of France or of Germany or of the United States, but only that by intelligence and character they are quite fitted to start on the road to responsible government, at least to such kind as was conceded for the first time to Canada, Australia, Italy, the Balkan States, Austria, Hungary, etc. The illiteracy of the masses may be a good reason for not introducing universal suffrage, but it is hardly a valid reason for refusing a kind of constitution which may place India in the same position, in the matter of responsible Government, as Great Britain, France, Austria-Hungary, Italy and the United States were when those countries showed the same percentage of illiteracy. Literacy has nowhere been the test of political power. Burma had almost no illiteracy when the British took possession of it; its population was absolutely homogeneous and the solidarity of the nation ran no risk from "cleavages of religion, race and caste." Even today Burma has the highest figures of literacy in the whole of British India. In that respect it occupies a higher position than Roumania, Bulgaria, Serbia, Greece, many of the Russian States and perhaps even Italy and Hungary and possibly some of the South American Republics. In the matter of race and religion, too, its position is better than that of the countries mentioned, yet the authors of the Report do not propose to concede to it even such beginnings of responsible government as they are prepared to grant to the other provinces of India. The fact is that mere literacy does not play an important part in the awakening of political consciousness in a people. It is a useful ingredient of character required for the exercise of political power but by no means essential.

POVERTY

The argument based on poverty is of still less force. On the other hand, it is the best reason why the people of India should have the power to determine and carry out their fiscal policy. We hope the admissions made in Paragraph 135 of the Report which we bodily reproduce [2] will once for all dispose of the silly statement, so often repeated even by men who ought to know better, that materially India has been highly

[2] "The Indian Government compiles no statistics showing the distribution of wealth, but such incomplete figures as we have obtained show that the number of persons enjoying a substantial income is very small. In one province the total number of persons who enjoy an income of £66 a year derived from other sources than land is 30,000; in another province 20,000. The revenue and rent returns also show how small the average agricultural holding is. According to one estimate, the number of landlords whose income derived from their proprietary holdings exceeds £20 a year in the United Provinces is about 126,000, out of a population of forty-eight millions. It is evident that the curve of wealth descends very steeply, and that enormous masses of the population have little to spare for more than the necessaries of life."

prosperous under British rule. If so, how is it that in the language of the Secretary of State for India and the Viceroy "enormous masses of the population have little to spare for more than the necessaries of life"? What about the prosperity of a province, one of the biggest in India (the United Provinces), in which the number of landlords (not tenants and farmers) whose income derived from their proprietary holdings exceeds £20 ($100 a year, which comes to 30 cents a day for the whole family), is about 126,000 out of a population of 48 millions!

Acceptance of the argument of poverty as sufficient to deprive people of political right is putting a premium on it which is hardly creditable to the political ethics of the twentieth century. It is the poorest and the most ignorant in the community who most egregiously suffer at the hands of autocracy. It is they who require protection from it. The wealthy and the educated know how to placate the bureaucrat and get what they want. It is the poor who pay the penalty of political helplessness, yet, curiously, it is for them and in their interest that the English Government in India proposes to withhold the power of the purse from the proposed Indian Councils and insists on denying the Indian people even the elements of responsible government. While we admit the general justice and accuracy of the observations made under the head of "extent of interest in political questions," "political capacity of the rural population," we fail to see anything in them which justifies the conclusion that the interests of the classes not politically minded will be safer in the hands of the British officer, and on the whole better protected by him than by his educated countrymen who are likely to get the power in case of responsible government being conceded now. In our judgment no greater argument for the immediate grant of a substantial step in the direction of complete responsible government throughout India and in all spheres of government, could be advanced than what is involved in the following observation of the authors of the joint Report:

"The rural classes have the greatest stake in the country because they contribute most to its revenues; but they are poorly equipped for politics and do not at present wish to take part in them. Among them are a few great landlords and a larger number of yeoman farmers. They are not ill-fitted to play a part in affairs, but with few exceptions they have not yet done so. But what is perhaps more important to appreciate than the mere content of political life in India is its rate of growth. No one who has observed Indian life during even the past five years can doubt that the growth is rapid and is real. It is beginning to affect the large landholders: here and there are signs of its beginning to affect even the villages. But recent events, and above all the war, have given it a new earnestness and a more practical character. Men are coming to realise more clearly that India's political future is not to be won merely by fine phrases: and that it depends on the capacity of her people themselves to face difficulties and to dispose of them. Hence comes the demand for compulsory education, for industries, for tariffs, for social reform, for social, public and even military service."

In the next paragraph, the authors approvingly give an extract from an official report in which it is frankly admitted that the rural population "may not be vocal, but they are certainly not voiceless." The last meeting of the Indian Congress was attended by

700 farmer delegates. Thousands of farmers have joined the Home Rule Leagues. The statement that "hitherto they have regarded the official as their representative in the Councils of the Government" is entirely devoid of any truth. In their eyes the official is the Government itself. Some of them may think that the official *represents* the Government, but to say that they regard the official as "*their representative* in the Councils of the Government" is a mere travesty of truth. The paragraph on the "interests of the ryot" bristles with so many unwarranted assumptions that we must enter an emphatic protest against its misleading nature.

But it gives us pleasure to accord our whole-hearted support to the following statement with which the paragraph opens:

> "It is just because the Indian ryot is inarticulate and has not been directly represented in our deliberations that we feel bound to emphasise the great claim he has upon our consideration. The figure of the individual cultivator does not often catch the eye of the Governments in Simla and Whitehall. It is chiefly in the mass that they deal with him, as a consumer of salt or of piece-goods, or unhappily too often as the victim of scarcity or disease."

It is true that "the district officer and his lieutenants" are in a position to know the difficulties that beset the ryot and his very human needs. But of what good is this knowledge of the district officer and his lieutenants to him if it has neither provided for the education of his children nor made any provision for his employment in occupations other than agriculture; nor saved him from the intricacies of the law;

nor protected him from the ubiquitous salt tax; nor raised his wages proportionately to the increase of prices; nor yet put him in a position to assert his human rights and to obtain redress for his human, too human, wrongs. If we examine a little more carefully the merits of what is claimed to have been done for him so far by "an official Government," we will find that the claim is by no means established.

We have no desire to deny that among the foreign officers of the British Government in India there are and have been a great many who were genuinely anxious to help the ryot and do all which is claimed to have been done for him in this paragraph, but that they have been unable to do anything worth mentioning will be admitted by every right-minded official.[3] The reasons for their failure were not of their making. The laws of the land made by the British legislators fresh from the Inns of Court, the spirit of the administration and the system of land taxation have effectively prevented them from doing many of the things which they might otherwise have liked to do. We are sorry that the eminent statesmen responsible for the report should have been the unconscious instruments of producing an entirely wrong impression by the statements in this paragraph. If the statements are true, India must be a veritable paradise and the lot of the Indian ryot enviable. But we know, and the authors of the Report knew it as well, and they have stated in so many words that it is not so. We can quote any number of authorities to show that the Indian ryot is the most pitiable figure in the whole

[3] See *Punjab in Peace and War*, by S. S. Thorborn, London, 1904.

length and breadth of India, if not in the whole world. This is not the place to quote the easily accessible opinions of eminently qualified and highly trustworthy British writers and adminstrators on the subject.[4] The English official Government has no doubt *professed* to do all it claims to have done for the ryot, but how far it has benefited him in these directions is another story. To ask credit for having provided him with a system of law "simple, cheap and certain," or for having established schools and dispensaries within reasonable distance of his residence; or for even having looked after his cattle, by the provision of grazing lands; or for having supplied wood for his implements is to run violently in the face of facts to the contrary. These are verily his principal complaints against British rule. The official Government is certainly entitled to some credit for having started the coöperative credit societies and a few coöperative rural banks for the benefit of the peasantry, but the reform is so belated and at present plays such an insignificant part in the rural economy of India that it seems hardly worth mentioning or discussing.[5]

But even assuming that the official Government has so far done all that for the ryot, what reason is there to insinuate that the Government of the people will fail to do it for him in the future or will not do it so well as or even better, than has been heretofore done by the bureaucracy? It is quite a gratuitous assumption that in future he will be required to do all these things for himself. Even in the most advanced

[4] They are collected in *England's Debt to India*, by the present author. New York, B. W. Huebsch, 1917.

[5] See Sir D. Hamilton, *Calcutta Review*, July, 1916.

democracies in the world the peasantry or the masses of the people do not do these things for themselves. Most of these things are done by officials. The only difference is that in a responsible government the officials are the servants of the people while in an absolute government they are their masters. We are really surprised at the presumption of the British bureaucrat, in posing as the special friend of the Indian masses as against their own educated countrymen. The experience of the past does not support the claim and there is absolutely no reason to assume that it will be different in the future. A mere cursory glance at the resolutions of the Indian National Congress passed continuously for a period of thirty years, will show how persistently and earnestly the educated classes have been pleading *inter alia* for (a) compulsory and free education, (b) for technical instruction in vocations, (c) for the reduction of the salt tax and the land tax, (d) for the raising of the minimum incomes liable to income tax, (e) for the provision of pasture lands, (f) for the comforts of the third-class railway travelling public, (g) for the milder administration of the forest laws, (h) for the reform of the Police, etc. All these years the bureaucracy did nothing for the ryot and now they pose as his special friends, whose continuance in power and in office is necessary for his protection from the politically minded middle classes. We are a friend neither of the landlord nor of the capitalist. We believe that the ryot and the working men in India as elsewhere are being exploited and robbed by the classes in possession of the means of production and distribution. We would wholeheartedly support any scheme which would open a way to a just and righteous distribution of wealth and land in India and which would insure the ryot and the working man his rightful place in the body politic. We would not mind the aid of the foreign bureaucracy toward that end if we could be sure that the bureaucracy would or could do it. But we have no doubts in the matter that it cannot be done. The bureaucracy has so far played into the hands of the plutocrat. They have served first their own capitalists and then the capitalists and landlords of India. Some among them have tried to do a little for the submerged classes, the poor ryot and the ill-paid sweated laborer, but their efforts were of no consequence. They have failed and their failure is writ large on the face of the ryot. We are not sanguine that the politically minded classes when they get power will immediately rehabilitate the ryot and give him his due. We have no hope of that kind. Yet we unhesitatingly support the demand of the politically minded classes for a responsible government in India. In our judgment, that is the only way to raise the masses to a consciousness of their rights and responsibilities. The experience of the West tells us that in that way and in that way alone lies salvation. Political consciousness must travel from the classes to the masses and the longer the inauguration of popular Government is delayed, the greater the delay in the awakening of the ryot and the working man. Absolutism must first give way and transfer its power to the politically minded classes, then will come the turn of the masses to demand their rights and compel compliance. We can see no risk of a greater harm or injury to the masses of India from the transference of power from the hands of a close bureaucracy of foreigners into the hands of the educated and propertied oligarchy of their own countrymen. Even in countries like Great Britain, America and France it is the educated and the propertied classes who rule. Why then this hubbub about the impropriety and danger of giving power to the same classes in India? Why are the representatives of landlordism and capitalism in the British House of Lords and among the ranks of Imperial Anglo-Indians so solicitous of the welfare of the Indian masses, when they have for so long persistently denied justice to the proletariat of their own country? It is a strange phenomenon to see the champions of privilege and status, the defenders of capitalism and landlordism, the advocates of the rights of property, the upholders of caste in Great Britain, spending so much powder and shot to *protect* the Indian ryot from the prospective exploitation of him by the Indian Brahmin and the Indian Banya [6] (the priest and the capitalist). Let the British Brahmin and the British Banya first begin by doing justice to the proletariat of their own country and then it will be time for them to convince the Indian of their altruism and honesty of purpose in obstructing the inauguration of responsible government in India in the interests of the Indian proletariat. In this connection the authors of the Report make some pertinent observations which deserve to be quoted. After speaking of "religious animosities and social cleavages" and the duty of discouraging them the authors say:

"Nor are we without hope that the reforms will themselves help to provide the remedy. We would not be misunderstood. Representative institutions

[6] "Banya" in Hindustan means "trader."

in the West, where all are equal at the ballot box, have checked but not abolished social exclusiveness. We do not make a higher claim for similar institutions in India than that they will help to soften the rigidity of the caste-system. But we hope that these incidents of it which lead to the permanent degradation and ostracism of the lowest castes will tend to disappear in proportion to the acceptance of the ideas on which the new constitution rests. There is a further point. An autocratic administration, which does not share the religious ideas of the people, obviously finds its sole safe ground in leaving the whole department of traditional social usage severely alone. In such matters as child-marriage, it is possible that through excess of caution proper to the regime under which it works, it may be actually perpetuating and stereotyping customs which the better mind of India might be brought, after the necessary period of stuggle, to modify. A government, in which Indians themselves participate, invigorated by a closer touch with a more enlightened popular opinion, may be able with all due caution to effect with the free assent or acquiescence of the Indians themselves, what under the present system has to be rigorously set aside."

Nor are the authors unmindful of the effect of free institutions on the character of the people as they themselves over and over again recognise.

"Free institutions have, as we have said, the faculty of reacting on the adverse conditions in which the start has to be made. The backwardness of education may embarrass the experiment at the outset; but it certainly ought not to stop it, because popular government in India as elsewhere is sure to promote the progressive spread of education and so a widening circle of improvement will be set up." [7]

[7] In this connection the pertinent observations of the AGA KHAN in his book *India in Transition* may be read (Chapter XXV), Putnam, New York.

Among the authors' reasons for what they call a gradual advance they state the following also: (a) "We find it freely and widely admitted that they (i.e. the Indians) are not yet ready." This admission may legitimately be used against the total withdrawal of all control of Indian affairs by the Parliament. Firstly, it is questionable whether any such admission is really "freely and widely" made. Secondly, the admission justifies the retention of the powers of vital, general supervision and general control and also the retention of some Europeans in the higher services, but not the total denial of all responsibility for maintaining law and order and of all power to control the central Executive. (b) That the responsibility of India's defence is the ultimate burden which rests on the Government of India; and this duty is the last which can be intrusted to inexperienced or unskilful hands.

"So long as India depends for her internal and external security upon the army and navy of the United Kingdom, the measure of self-determination which she enjoys must be inevitably limited. We cannot think that Parliament would consent to the employment of British arms in support of a policy over which it had no control and of which it might disapprove. The defence of India is an Imperial question: and for this reason the Government of India must retain both the power and the means of discharging its responsibilities for the defence of the country and to the Empire as a whole."

The defence of India involves, (a) men for the army and the navy, (b) officers, (c) war materials and war ships, (d) experts in strategy, (e) money. That India pays for her defense and also contributes towards the defence of the Empire are facts which cannot be questioned. That she shall continue to do so in the future may also be assumed. That it is extremely desirable that in the matter of war supplies she should be self-dependent has been freely admitted. The permanent Indian army as constituted in pre-war days contained two-thirds Indians and one-third British. If the present strength of the Indian army be examined it will be found that the proportion of British troops is still smaller. There is absolutely no need of British soldiers in India for the purposes of defence, but if the British Government wants to keep them as safeguards against mutiny among the purely Indian army or against the spirit of rebellion that at any time may exhibit itself among the Indian people, then the British exchequer must pay for them as it did in the case of British garrison in South Africa or as the United States does in the case of American troops in the Philippines. It is adding insult to injury to argue that we should not only pay for British troops but that the fact that British troops form a constituent element of the Indian army should be used against us for denying us full responsibility even in civil affairs. The armies of the various Asiatic Governments surrounding India have no European elements in them and the Indian soldier is as efficient a fighter as is needed as a protection. That the Indian army should be almost exclusively officered by the British is a survival of the policy of mistrust, jealousy and racial discrimination which has hitherto prevailed. It is time that the Indian army should in future be mainly officered by the Indians. Until that is achieved it must continue as a tentative measure to be officered by the British, and the Indian Revenues must bear the burden. But that is hardly any reason for denying us full responsible government even on the civil side. The Indians do not desire nor demand the transfer of the control over the Army or the Navy until the Army is principally officered by the Indians and an Indian Navy has been built to supplement the Imperial Navy. From this criticism of the reasons advanced by the authors for a very mild "advance" (called "gradual") it is with pleasure that we turn to the brighter side of the picture showing the favorable features of the situation. The position of the educated Indian is described fairly and squarely in Paragraph 140.

"The old assumption that the interests of the ryot must be confided to official hands is strenuously denied by modern educated Indians. They claim that the European official must by his lack of imagination and comparative lack of skill in tongues be gravely handicapped in interpreting the thoughts and desires of an Asiatic people. . . . Our educational policy in the past aimed at satisfying the few, who sought after English education, without sufficient thought of the consequences which might ensue from not taking care to extend instruction to the many. We have in fact created a limited *intelligentsia*, who desire advance; and we cannot stay their progress entirely until education has been extended to the masses. It has been made a reproach to the educated classes that they have followed too exclusively after one or two pursuits, the law, journalism or school teaching: and that these are all callings which make men inclined to overrate the importance of words and phrases. But even if there is substance in the count, we must take note also how far the past policy of Government is responsible. We have not succeeded in making education practical.

It is only now, when the war has revealed the importance of industry, that we have deliberately set about encouraging Indians to undertake the creation of wealth by industrial enterprise, and have thereby offered the educated classes any tangible inducement to overcome their traditional inclination to look down on practical forms of energy. We must admit that the educated Indian is a creation peculiarly of our own; and if we take the credit that is due to us for his strong points we must admit a similar liability for his weak ones. Let us note also in justice to him that the progressive Indian appears to realise the narrow basis of his position and is beginning to broaden it. In municipal and university work he has taken a useful and creditable share. We find him organising effort not for political ends alone, but for various forms of public and social service. He has come forward and done valuable work in relieving famine and distress by floods, in keeping order at fairs, in helping pilgrims, and in promoting co-operative credit. Although his ventures in the fields of commerce have not been always fortunate, he is beginning to turn his attention more to the improvement of agriculture and industry. Above all, he is active in promoting education and sanitation; and every increase in the number of educated people adds to his influence and authority."

The authors also say:

"We must remember, too, that the educated Indian has come to the front by hard work; he has seized the education which we offered him because he first saw its advantages; and it is he who has advocated and worked for political progress. All this stands to his credit. For thirty years he has developed in his Congress and latterly in the Muslim League free popular convocations which express his ideals. We owe him sympathy because he has conceived and pursued the idea of managing his own affairs, an aim which no Englishman can fail to respect. He has made a skilful, and on the whole a moderate, use of the opportunities which we have given him in the legislative councils of influencing Government and affecting the course of public business, and of recent years, he has by speeches and in the press done much to spread the idea of a united and self-respecting India among thousands who had no such conception in their minds. Helped by the inability of the other classes in India to play a prominent part he has assumed the place of leader; but his authority is by no means universally acknowledged and may in an emergency prove weak."

In face of these observations about the politically minded classes of India it is rather unkind of the authors to insinuate later on that in the interests of the foreign merchant, the foreign missionary and the European servants of the state it is necessary that the Government of India should yet remain absolute and that, in the provinces as well, important branches of the administration should be excluded from the jurisdiction of the popular assemblies.

To sum up, while we are prepared to concede that the conditions of the problem may justify the withholding of absolute autonomy, — political, fiscal, and military, — for some time, there is nothing in them which can in any way be deemed sufficient to deny full political, and, if not complete, at least substantial fiscal autonomy to the Indian people at once.

VI

THE PUBLIC SERVICES IN INDIA

> The governing consideration, therefore, in all these cases [speaking of German colonies] must be that the inhabitants should be placed under the control of an administration acceptable to themselves, one of whose main purposes will be to prevent their exploitation for the benefit of European capitalists or Governments.
>
> DAVID LLOYD GEORGE
>
> "The War Aims of the Allies." Speech delivered to delegates of the Trades Unions, at the Central Hall, Westminster, January 5, 1918.

UNTIL now the European servants of the British Government have ruled India quite autocratically. The powers delegated to and the discretion vested in them have been so large that they could do almost anything they liked. They could make or mar the fortunes of millions; they could further their happiness or add to their misery by the simple fiat of their will. The only limitation on their power was their own sense of duty and justice. That some of them did let themselves go is no wonder. The wonder is that the instances of unbridled oppression and tyranny were not more numerous than they have actually been. Speaking of the European services generally, we have nothing but admiration for their general character. The particular branch of the Public Services that has been all along entrusted with the general administration of the country is known as the Indian Civil Service. It is recruited in England and is overwhelmingly European in personnel. On April 1, 1913, only forty-six of the 1319 civilians on the *cadre* were natives of India.

Speaking of the executive organizations that have so far ruled India, the eminent authors of the Report for the reorganization of the Government of India remark that it may "well be likened to a mere system of official posts, actuated *till* now by impulses of its own, but affected by the popular ideas which impinge on it from three sources — the British Parliament, the legislative councils and the local boards." The sentence would have been correct if in place of "but affected" the authors had said "and affected but little." "The system," they add, "has in the main depended for its effectiveness on the experience, wisdom and energy of the services themselves. It has, for the most part, been represented by the Indian Civil Service which, though having little to do with the technical departments of government, *has for over* 100 *years in practice had the administration entrusted to its hands, because, with the exception of the offices of the Governor General, Governors, and some members of the executive councils, it has held practically all the places involving superior control.* It has been in effect much more of a government corporation than of a purely civil service in the English sense. It has been made a reproach to the Indian Civil Service that it regards itself as the Government; but a view which strikes the critic familiar with parliamentary government as arrogant is little more than a condensed truth." [The italics are ours.]

The Indian Civil Service has thus developed all the characteristics, good and bad, of a caste. It has been a powerful bureaucracy, as exclusive, proud, arrogant and self-sufficient, — if not even more so, — as the original Brahmin oligarchy of the land, except that while the Brahmin oligarchy had ties of race, religion and culture with the rest of the population, the Indian Civil Service is almost entirely composed of aliens. The ancient Brahmins were, however, kept in check by the military caste. The mutual jealousies of these two castes afforded some kind of protection to the people in general. But in the case of the British Indian Civil Service, the military have given entire support to their civilian fellow-countrymen and have been completely under their will.

The Brahmins of India have left a monumental record of their labors. They produced great thinkers, writers, legislators, administrators and organizers. In their own time they were as wise, energetic and resourceful as any bureaucracy in the world has ever been or will ever be. Yet the system of life they devised cut at the roots of national vitality. It dried almost all the springs of corporate national life. It reduced the bulk of the population to a position of complete subservience to their will, of blind faith in their wisdom, of absolute dependence on their initiative. It deprived the common people of all opportunities of independent thought and independent action. It brought about a kind of national atrophy. And this, in spite of the fact that they began by imposing a rigorous code of self-denial on themselves and their class. For themselves they wanted nothing but a life of poverty and asceticism. Their economic interests were never in theory or in practice in conflict with those of the rest of the body politic.

A Brahmin was forbidden to engage in trade or otherwise accumulate wealth. His life was a life of strict self-abnegation. This cannot be said of the Indian Civil Servant. He receives a handsome salary for his services, expects and receives periodic promotion until he reaches a position which, from an economic point of view, is not unenviable. After retirement he is free to engage in trade and otherwise accumulate wealth. But over and above this, what distinguishes an Indian Civil Servant from an old Brahmin bureaucrat is the fact that in India he represents a nation whose economic interest may not always be in harmony with those of the people of India. He is thus supposed to be the guardian of the interests of his countrymen, and is expected to further them as much as he can without altogether endangering the safety of British rule in India. Looked at from this angle, we have no hesitation in saying that the work of the Indian Civil Service, too, has in its way, been monumental. As a rule, they have proved capable administrators, individually honest, hardworking and alert. They have organized and tabulated India in a way, perhaps, never done before. But after all has been said in their praise, it cannot be denied that they have done India even more harm than the Brahmin oligarchy in its time, did, by the support they lent to economic exploitation of the country by men of their own race and religion. Now, in this latter respect, we want to guard against being misunderstood. The Indian Civil Service has, in the course of about a century, produced a fairly good number of men who have honestly and fearlessly stood for the protection of Indian interests against those of people of their own race and religion. In doing so they have sometimes ruined their own prospects of promotion and advancement. Whenever they failed in their self-imposed task, and more often they failed than not, they failed because the authorities at the top were forced by considerations of domestic and imperial policy to do otherwise. On the whole, the defects of the bureaucratic administration were more the defects of the system than of the individuals composing it.

The Indian Civil Servant, like the old Brahmin, is autocratic and dictatorial. He dislikes any display of independence by the people put under his charge. He discourages initiative. He likes to be called and considered the *Mai bap* (mother and father) of his subjects. On those who literally consider him such he showers his favors. The others he denounces and represses. This has, in the course of time, led to national emasculation. That is our chief complaint against the Indian Civil Service. Of the other services we would rather not speak. They have by no means been so pure and high-minded as the I. C. S., nor perhaps so autocratic and dictatorial. The number of men who misused their powers and opportunities to their own advantage has been much larger in services other than the I. C. S. Yet they all have done a certain amount of good work for India; whether one looks at the engineering works designed and executed by them, or the researches they have made in the science of healing and preventing disease, or the risks they have run in preserving order or maintaining peace one cannot but admire their efficiency and ability. The grievances of the Indian Nationalists against the Public Services in India may be thus summarized:

(*a*) That the services monopolize too much power and are practically uncontrolled by and irresponsible to the people of the country.

(*b*) That the higher branches of the services contain too many foreigners.

(*c*) That these are recruited in England, and from some of them the Indians are altogether barred.

(*d*) That even when doing the same work Indians are not paid on the same scale as the Europeans.

(*e*) That the Government has often kept on men of proved inefficiency and of inferior qualities.

(*f*) That, considering the economic conditions of India, the higher servants of the Government are paid on a scale unparalleled in the history of public administration in the world.

(*g*) That the interests of the services often supersede those of the country and the Government.

(*h*) And last, but not least, that by the gathering of all powers of initiative and execution in their hands they have emasculated India.

As regards (*a*) we have already quoted the opinion of the eminent authors of the report. The principle laid down in the announcement of August 20, and the scheme proposed are supposed to do away with the element of irresponsibility. It is obvious that with the introduction of the principle of popular control into the Government, the power of individual servants of the executive will not remain what it is now, or has been in the past. Much that is vested in and done by the service will be transferred to public bodies elected by popular vote. This will naturally affect (*b*) and (*c*) also. We will here stop to quote again from the Report:

"In the forefront of the announcement of August 20 the policy of the increasing association of Indians in every branch of the administration was definitely placed. It has not been necessary for us, nor indeed would it have been possible, to go into this large question in detail in the time available for our inquiry. We have already seen that Lord Hardinge's Government was anxious to increase the number of Indians in the public services, and that a Royal Commission was appointed in 1912 to examine and report on the existing limitations in the employment of Indians. . . . The report was signed only a few months after the outbreak of war, and its publication was deferred in the hope that the war would not be prolonged. When written, it might have satisfied moderate Indian opinion, but when published two years later it was criticised as wholly disappointing. Our inquiry has since given us ample opportunity of judging the importance which Indian opinion attaches to this question. While we take account of this attitude, a factor which carries more weight with us is that since the report was signed an entirely new policy toward Indian government has been adopted, which must be very largely dependent for success on the extent to which it is found possible to introduce Indians into every branch of the administration."

The authors of the Report then proceed to state the limitations of the process, subject to the general remark that at the present moment there are few Indians (we do not admit this) trained in public life, who can replace the Europeans, and thus to alter the personnel of a service must be a long and steady process. They admit that:

"If responsible government is to be established in India there will be a far greater need than is even dreamt of at present for persons to take part in public affairs in the legislative assemblies and elsewhere; and for this reason the more Indians we can employ in the public services the better. Moreover, it would lessen the burden of Imperial responsibilities if a body of capable Indian administrators could be produced. We regard it as necessary, therefore, that recruitment of a largely increased proportion of Indians should be begun at once."

In the next paragraph they state why, in their judgment, it is necessary that a substantial portion of the services must continue to be European. Their reasons may be gathered from the following:

"The characteristics which we have learned to associate with the Indian public services must as far as possible be maintained and the leaven of officers possessed of them should be strong enough to assure and develop them in the service as a whole. The qualities of courage, leadership, decision, fixity of purpose, detached judgment and integrity in her public servants will be as necessary as ever to India. There must be no such sudden swamping of any service with any new element that its whole character suffers a rapid alteration."

On these grounds they make the following recommendations:

"I. That all distinctions based on race be removed, and that appointments to all branches of the public service be made without racial discrimination" (Paragraph 315).

"II. That for all the public services, for which there is recruitment in England open to Europeans and Indians alike, there must be a system of appointment in India, . . . and we propose to supplement it by fixing a definite percentage of recruitment to be made in India."

"III. We have not been able to examine the question of the percentage of recruitment to be made in India for any service other than the Indian Civil Service. The Commission recommended that 25 per cent. of the superior posts of that service should be recruited for in India. We consider that changed conditions warrant some increase in that proportion, and we suggest that 33 per cent. of the superior posts should be recruited for in India, and that this percentage should be increased by 1½ per cent. annually until the periodic commission is appointed which will re-examine the whole subject. . . . We have dealt only with the Indian Civil Service, but our intention is that there should be in all other services now recruited from England a fixed percentage of recruitment in India, increasing annually."

Now we must admit that this is certainly a distinct and marked advance on the existing situation. The Indian Constitutional party, however, wants to have the percentage of recruitment in India fixed at 50 per cent., retaining at the same time the annual increase suggested. In our opinion, this difference is not material, provided the number of posts to which the rule of percentage is to be applied is substantially reduced. We may state our position briefly.

We are of the opinion that the system of administration in India is much more costly than it should be, considering the sources and the amounts of Indian revenues. Unless the industries of the country are developed we can see no new sources of increased taxation. Consequently, to us, it seems essential that some economy should be effected in the various departments of the administration. The only way to effect that economy is to substantially reduce the number of posts on which it is considered necessary to retain a certain percentage of Europeans. In speaking of the machinery of the Government of India, the authors of the Report say:

"*We think we have reason for saying that in some respects the machinery is no longer equal to the needs of the time.* The normal work of the departments is heavy. The collective responsibility of the Government is weighty, especially in time of war. There is little time or energy left for those activities of a political nature which the new situation in the country demands. A legislative session of the Government of India imposes a serious strain upon the departments, and especially on the members in charge of them. But apart from the inevitable complexities of the moment, the growing burden of business, which results from the changing political conditions of the country, is leading to an accumulation of questions which cannot be disposed of as quickly as they present themselves. We find the necessity for reforms admitted, principles agreed upon, and decisions taken, and then long delays in giving effect to them. Difficulties are realized, enquiries are started, commissions report, and then there is a pause. There is a belief abroad that assurances given in public pronouncement of policy are sometimes not fulfilled. On this occasion, therefore, we have taken steps to guard against such imputations, and to provide means for ensuring the ordered development of our plans."

PRESENT CAUSES OF DELAY

"267. The main fault for the clogging of the machine does not, we think, lie altogether with its highly trained engineers. What is chiefly wanted is some change of system in the directions of simplicity and speed. *How does it happen that announcements are made that arouse expectations only to defeat them?* We know that it is not from any intention of deluding the public. We suggest that it is because the wheels move too slowly for the times; the need for change is realized, but because an examination of details would take too long, promises are made in general terms, which on examination it becomes necessary so to qualify with reservations as to disappoint anticipations, and even to lead to charges of breach of faith. We suspect that a root-cause of some political discontent lies in such delays. Now, so far as the provinces are concerned, we believe that our proposals *for freeing them to a great extent from the control of the Government of India and the Secretary of State will improve matters. But the Government of India are in the worst case.*" [The italics are ours.]

These observations raise an apprehension in our mind that it is proposed to add to the strength of the services under the Government of India. We, for ourselves, do not see how it can be otherwise. With the steady admission of the popular element into the Government of India the activities of the latter are likely to increase rather than diminish; the secretarial work of the different departments will expand rather than contract. The question of questions is how to meet the increased cost.

The remedy is the same as was suggested many years ago by Sir William Hunter, the official historian of India. He said:

"If we are to give a really efficient administration to India, many services must be paid for at lower rates even at present. For those rates are regulated in the higher branches of the administration by the cost of officers brought from England. You cannot work with imported labor as cheaply as you can with native labor, and I regard the more extended employment of the natives, not only as an act of justice, but as a financial necessity. If we are to govern the Indian people efficiently and cheaply, we must govern them by means of themselves, and pay for the administration at the market rates for native labor."

Now, whatever may be said about the necessity of maintaining a strong European element in the departments which require initiative, courage, resourcefulness and all the other qualities of "leadership" they are certainly not a *sine qua non* for efficiency in secretarial work. We can see no reason why, then, the different secretariats of the Government of India cannot be manned mainly, if not exclusively, by Indians. Their salaries need not be the same as those now paid to the Europeans engaged in these departments. May we ask if there is any country on earth where such high salaries are paid to the secretarial heads of departments as in India? Secretaries to the Government of India in the Army and Public works and Legislative departments receive 42,000 Rs. each ($14,000, or £2800 a year); Secretaries to the Government of India in the Finance, Foreign, Home, Revenue, Agriculture, Commerce and Industry and Education departments get Rs. 48,000 a year each ($16,000 or £3,200); Educational Commissioners from 30 to 36,000 Rs. ($10,000 to $12,000).

These secretarial officers are not of Cabinet rank. Besides their salaries they get various allowances, and the purchasing value of the rupee in India is much higher than that of 33 cents in the United States or of 16d. in the United Kingdom, the exchange equivalents of an Indian rupee. The same remarks may be made about Provincial Secretariats. We do not ignore the fact that a European who cuts himself away from his country and people for the best part of his life cannot be expected to give his time, energy and talents for the compensation he might accept in his own country, nor that, if the best kind of European talent is desired for India, the compensation must be sufficiently attractive to tempt competent men to accept it. In Paragraphs 318 to 322, both inclusive, the Secretary of India and the Viceroy have put forward a forceful plea for improvement in the conditions of the European Services by (*a*) increment in their salaries, (*b*) expediting promotions, and (*c*) grant of additional allowances, and also by bettering the prospects of pensions and leave. We are afraid the only way to obtain the concurrence of Indian public opinion in this matter, if at all, is by restricting the number of posts which *must* be held by Europeans. The *cadre* of services to which the rule of percentage is to apply must be reduced in strength, and if Europeans are required for posts outside these they should be employed for short periods and from an open market. For example, it seems inconceivable to us why professional men like doctors, engineers and professors should be recruited for permanent service. Nor is there any reason why the recruitment should be confined to persons of British domicile. The Government of India must be run on business principles. With the exception, perhaps, of the higher posts in the I. C. S. and in the

Army, all other offices should be filled by taking the supply on the best available terms for short periods and from open market. By reducing the number of higher posts to which the rule of percentage should apply, the Government would be reducing the number of Indian officers who could claim the same salary as is given to their European colleagues. In our humble opinion, the latter claim is purely sentimental, and the best interests of the country require that the administration should be as economical as is compatible with efficiency. The strength of the different permanent services should be reduced as much as possible and the deficiency made up by the appointment of the best persons available at the price which the administration may be willing to pay, whether such persons be European, Indian or American. Take the Indian Educational Service, for example. The members start with a salary of 6000 Rs. a year ($2000 or £400) and rise to about 24,000 Rs. a year ($8000 or £1600). In the United States, to the best of our knowledge, few professors, if any, get a salary higher than $7000 or 21,000 Rs. a year. High-class graduates of Harvard, Yale and Columbia start their tutorial careers at $2000 to $3000 a year, many at $1500 a year. These men would refuse to go to India on a similar salary. On the other hand, if a salary of $4000 to $10,000 were offered to a select few, the services of *the men at the top* might be had for a short period. Surely, in the best interests of education, it is much better to get first-class men on high salaries for short periods than permanently to have third-class men beginning with smaller salaries and eventually rising to high salaries and ensuring to themselves life long pensions. What is true of the Educational Service is similarly, if not equally, true of the Medical, the Engineering and other scientific services. At the present time we have men in these technical services who received their education about twenty or twenty-five years ago and whose knowledge of their respective sciences is antiquated and rusty. Apothecaries, absolutely innocent of any knowledge of modern surgery, are often appointed to the post of Civil Surgeons. No sensible Indian desires that the present incumbents should be interfered with, except where it is possible to retire them under the terms of their service. All engagements should be met honorably. What is needed is that in future there should be a radical departure in the practice of appointing non-Indians to responsible posts in India. We do not want to deprive ourselves of the privilege of being guided in our work by European talent, nor should we grudge them adequate compensation for their services. What we object to is (1) racial discrimination; (2) excessive power being vested in individual officers; (3) the employment of more than a necessary number of persons of alien origin; (4) the crippling of the country's resources by burdening its finances with unnecessary pensions and leave allowances; (5) the continuance of men on service lists long after their usefulness has disappeared; (6) the filling of appointments by jobbery, as is now done in the so-called non-regulation provinces. We, in the Punjab, have been "blessed" by the rule of several generations of Smiths, Harrys and Jones. Those who failed to pass the I. C. S. joined the *cadre* by the back door and received the same emoluments as those who entered it by competition. It is they who block the avenues of promotions and not the sons of the soil.

COST OF ADMINISTRATION

On the subject of the cost of administration it will be instructive to compare the annual salaries allowed to the highest public servants in India, the United States and Japan.

The President of the United States, who ranks with the great royalties of the world in position, gets a salary of $75,000, without any other allowance. The Prime Minister of Japan gets 12,000 yen, or $6000. The Viceroy and the Governor General of India gets 250,000 rupees, or $83,000, besides a very large amount in the shape of various allowances. The Cabinet Ministers of the United States get a salary of $12,000 each, the Japanese 8000 yen or $4000, and the Members of the Viceroy's Council, $26,700 each.

In the whole Federal Government of the United States there are only three offices which carry a salary of more than $8000. They are:

The President of the General Navy Board	$13,500
Solicitor General	$10,000
Assistant Solicitor General	$9,000

All the other salaries range from $2100 to $8000. In the State Department all offices, including those of the secretaries, carry salaries of from $2100 to $5000. In the Treasury Department the Treasurer gets $8000, three other officers having $6000 each. All the remaining officials get from $2500 to $5000. In the War Department there are only two offices which have a salary of $8000 attached: that of Chief of

Staff and that of Quartermaster General. The rest get from $2000 to $6000. In the Navy Department, besides the President of the General Board mentioned above, the President of the Naval Examination Board gets $8000 and so does the Commandant of the Marine Corps. All the rest get from $6000 downwards. In the Department of Agriculture there is only one office carrying a salary of $6000. All the rest get from $5000 downwards. The Chief of the Weather Bureau, an expert, gets $6000. In the Commerce Department four experts get $6000 each, the rest from $5000 downwards.

In Japan the officials of the Imperial Household have salaries ranging from $2750 to $4000. Officials of the Higher Civil Service get from $1850 to $2100 a year; the Vice-Minister of State, $2500; Chief of the Legislative Bureau, $2500; the Chief Secretary of the Cabinet, $2500; and the Inspector General of the Metropolitan Police, $2500; President of the Administrative Litigation Court, $3000; President of the Railway Board, $3750; President of the Privy Council, $3000; Vice-President of the Privy Council, $2750, and so on.

When we come to India we find that the President of the Railway Board gets from $20,000 to $24,000 and that two other members of the Railway Board get $16,000. Secretaries in the Army, Public Works, and Legislative Departments get $14,000. Secretaries in Finance, Foreign, Home, Revenue, Agriculture, Commerce and Industry Departments get $16,000. The Secretary in the Education Department gets $12,000; Joint Secretary, $10,000; Controller and Auditor-General, $14,000; Accountant-General, from

$9,000 to $11,000; Commissioner of Salt Revenue, $10,000; Director of Post and Telegraph, from $12,000 to $14,000.

Among the officers directly under the Government of India there are only a few who get salaries below $7000. Most of the others get from that sum up to $12,000.

The United States includes forty-eight States and territories. Some of them are as large in area, if not even larger, than the several provinces of India. The Governors of these States are paid from $2500 to $12,000 a year. Illinois is the only State paying $12,000; five States, including New York and California, pay $10,000; two, Massachusetts and Indiana, pay $8000; one pays $7000, and three pay $6000. All the rest pay $5000 or less. There is only one territory, the Philippines, which pays a salary of $20,000 to its Governor-General.

In India the Governors of Madras, Bombay and Bengal each receive $40,000, besides a large amount for allowances. The Lieutenant-Governors of the Punjab, the United Provinces, Bihar and Burma get $33,000 each, besides allowances. The Chief Commissioners receive $11,000 in Bihar, $18,700 in Assam, $20,700 in the Central Provinces, and $12,000 in Delhi. The Political Residents in the native States receive from $11,000 to $16,000, besides allowances.

In Japan the governors of provinces are paid from $1850 to $2250 per year, besides allowances varying from $200 to $300.

The Provincial services in India are paid on a more lavish scale than anywhere else in the world. In Bengal the salaries range from $1600 for Assistant

Magistrate and Collector to $21,333 to Members of the Council, and this same extravagance is also true of the other provinces.

Coming to the Judiciary, we find that Justices of the Supreme Court of the United States get a salary of $14,500 each, the Chief Justice getting $15,000; the Circuit Judges get a salary of $7000 each; the District Judges, $6000. In the State of New York the Judges of the Supreme Court, belonging to the General Sessions, get from $17,500 and those of the Special Sessions from $9000 to $10,000 each. City Magistrates get from $7000 to $8000. In India the Chief Justice of Bengal gets $24,000; the Chief Justices of Bombay, Madras and the United Provinces, $20,000 each. The Chief Judges of the Chief Court of the Punjab and Burma get $16,000 each and the Puisine Judges of the High Courts the same amounts.

The Puisine Judges of the Chief Courts receive $14,000. In the Province of Bengal the salaries of the District and Session Judges range from $8,000 to $12,000. District Judges of the other provinces get from about $7000 to $12,000. The Deputy Commissioners in India get a salary in the different provinces ranging from $6000 to $9000 a year. The Commissioners get from $10,000 to $12,000.

In Japan the Appeal Court Judges and Procurators get from $900 to $2500 a year. Only one officer, the President of the Court of Causation, gets as much as $3000. The District Court Judges and Procurators are paid at the rate of from $375 to $1850. It is needless to compare the salaries of minor officials in the three countries. Since the Indian taxpayer has to pay so heavily for the European services engaged in the work of administration, it is necessary that even Indian officers should be paid on a comparatively high scale, thus raising the cost of administration hugely and affecting most injuriously the condition of the men in the lower grades of the government service. The difference between the salaries of the officers and the men forming the rank and file of the government in the three countries shows clearly how the lowest ranks in India suffer from the fact that the highest governmental officials are paid at such high rates.

In New York City the Chief Inspector gets $3500 a year; Captains, $2750; Lieutenants, $2250; Surgeons, $1,750; and Patrolmen, $1,400 each. In Japan the Inspector General of the Metropolitan Police gets $2500. The figures of the lower officials are not available. But the minimum salary of a Constable is $6.50 a month, besides which he gets his equipment, uniform and boots free. In India the Inspectors General get from $8000 to $12,000, the Deputy Inspectors General from $6000 to $7200, District Superintendents of Police from $2666 to $4800, Assistants from $1200 to $2000, Inspectors from $600 to $1000, Sub-inspectors from $200 to $400, Head Constables from $60 to $80, Constables from $40 to $48.

We have taken these figures from the *Indian Year Book*, published by the *Times of India*, Bombay. We know as a fact that the Police-Constables in the Punjab are paid from $2.67 to $3.33 per month — that is, from $32 to $40 per year. The reader should mark the difference between the grades of salaries from the highest to the lowest in India as compared with the United States and Japan. While in India the lowest officials are frightfully underpaid, the highest grades are paid on a lavish scale. In the other countries of the world this is not the case.

EDUCATIONAL DEPARTMENT

In the United States (we quote the figures of New York) the lowest grade school teachers get a salary of $720, rising to $1500 a year. In the upper grades salaries range from $1820 to $2260. Principals of elementary schools receive $3500 and assistants $2500. In the High Schools salaries range from $900 to $3150, in training schools from $1000 to $3250. Principals of High Schools and Training Schools receive $5000 and the same salary is paid to the District Superintendent. The Commissioner of Education in New York gets $7500.

In Japan the Minister of Education, who is a Cabinet Minister, gets $4000, and the lowest salaries paid to teachers range from $8 to $9 per month. In the United States College Professors make from $3000 to $5000 per year, a few only getting higher sums. In Japan salaries range from $300 to $2000. Coming to India we find that while the Administrative officials and even the College Professors get fairly high salaries, the teachers in the schools are miserably underpaid.

Even the *Times of India*, an Anglo-Indian newspaper published in Bombay, has recently commented on the colossal difference between the salaries allowed at the top and those allowed at the bottom. Yet recently the Secretary of State has been sanctioning higher leave allowances to the European officers of the Indian Army.

The Secretary of State for India in Council has approved, with effect from January 1, 1919, the following revised rates of leave pay for officers of the Indian Army and Indian Medical service granted leave out of India:

INDIAN ARMY

	per annum
On appointment	£200
After completion of 3 years' service	250
" " 6 " "	300
" " 9 " "	350
" " 12 " "	400
" " 15 " "	450
" " 18 " "	500
" " 21 " "	550
" " 24 " "	600
" " 27 " "	650
" " 29 " "	700

INDIAN MEDICAL SERVICE.

On appointment	300
After completion of 3 years' service	350
" " 6 " "	400
" " 9 " "	450
" " 12 " "	500
" " 15 " "	550
" " 18 " "	600
" " 21 " "	650
" " 24 " "	700

VII

THE INDIAN ARMY AND NAVY

The real enemy is the war spirit fostered in Prussia. It is an ideal of a world in which force and brutality reign supreme, as against a world, an ideal of a world, peopled by free democracies, united in an honourable league of peace.

DAVID LLOYD GEORGE

"The Destruction of a False Ideal." Speech delivered at the Albert Hall on the launching of the New War Economy Campaign, October 22, 1917.

When the Indian troops first arrived in October, 1914, the situation was of so drastic a nature that it was necessary to call upon them at once to re-enforce the fighting front and help to stem the great German thrust. Their fine fighting qualities, tenacity, and endurance were well manifested during the first Battle of Ypres before they had been able to completely reorganize after their voyage from India.

LORD FRENCH, the First Commander-in-Chief of British forces on the Western front.

The full story of the Palestine victory still remained to be told, BUT WHEN THE RECORD OF THAT GLORIOUS CAMPAIGN WAS UNFOLDED, ACROSS THE PAGE OF HISTORY WOULD BE WRIT LARGE THE NAME OF INDIA.

LORD CHELMSFORD, the Governor-General of India, on September 26, 1918.

As is usual in our history, we have triumphed after many sad blunders and in the end we have defeated Turkey almost single-handed, though our main forces have throughout the war been engaged with another foe. In fact, IT IS TO INDIA THAT OUR RECENT VICTORY IS DUE. . . .

MAJOR GENERAL SIR FREDERICK MAURICE in *The New York Times*, November 6, 1918.

The present Governor of the Punjab (his precise designation is Lieutenant Governor), who is the most reactionary, self-complacent and conceited of all the provincial rulers of India, has in the course of his appeals for recruits for the present war said more than once that the right of self-government carries with it the responsibility of defending the country. The distinguished authors of the Report have also remarked in one place that so long as the duty of defending India rests on Great Britain, the British Parliament must control the Government of India. Now let us see what the facts are.

(1) The first thing to be remembered in this connection is that during the whole period of British rule in India, not a penny has been spent by Great Britain for Indian defence. The defence of India has been well provided for by Indian Revenues. On the other hand India has paid millions in helping Great Britain not only in defending the Empire, but in extending

it.[1] Whatever protection has been afforded to India by the British Navy — and that has by no means been small — has been more than repaid by India's services to the Empire in China, Egypt, South Africa and other parts of the world. As to the military forces of India, they consist of two wings: (*a*) the British and (*b*) the Indian. The pre-war Indian army consisted of 80,000 British and 160,000 Indians. Indian public opinion has for decades been protesting against the denial to Indians of officers' commissions in the Indian army, as also against the strength of the British element therein. Every British unit of the Indian army from the Field Marshal to the Tommy is paid for his services by India. India pays for these services not only during the time they form part of the Indian army but also for their training and equipment. It pays all their leave, transfer and pension charges. It even pays for whatever provision is made in England for their medical relief, etc. In the line of the military and naval defence of India, Great Britain has not done as much for India as she has done for the dominions and self-governing colonies. Under the circumstances it is adding insult to injury to insinuate that India has in any way shirked the duty of providing for her defence. We will say nothing of India's services during the war.

In the military defence of India, the contribution of the Punjab has always been the greatest. If the British provinces are considered singly, it will be found that the Punjab has been supplying the largest number of units for the Indian army, not only in the

[1] See chapter on "How India has helped England make her Empire," in *England's Debt to India*, by the present author.

ranks of the fighters, but also in the ranks of auxiliaries. During this war, too, the Punjab made the largest contribution of both combatants and non-combatants. Yet, if we compare the civil status of the people of the Punjab with that of other provinces, we will find that they have been persistently denied equality of status with Bengal, Bombay and Madras. The Punjab peasantry, which supplies the largest number of soldiers to the army, is the most illiterate and ignorant of all the classes of Indian population. Their economic and legal position may better be studied in Mr. Thorborn's *The Punjab in Peace and in War.* The Municipal and Local Boards of the province do not possess as much independence as has been conceded in the other provinces. The judicial administration of the province is as antiquated as it could possibly be under British rule. Instead of a High Court we have still a Chief court.[2] Captains and Majors and Colonels are still performing judicial functions as magistrates and judges. The trial by jury in the cases of Indians is unknown. Until lately the Punjab was stamped with the badge of inferioity by being called a non-Regulation province. Even in this report the Secretary of State for India and the Viceroy have spoken of it as a backward province. It will thus be seen that the contribution of the Punjab to the military strength of the Empire has in no way benefited her population in getting better opportunities for civil progress or greater civil liberties. But recently the President of the Punjab Provincial Conference uttered hard words against the Provincial administration's policy of repression and coercion. He said that their "cup of disappointment,

[2] It has now been converted into a High Court.

discontent and misery, in the Punjab, at any rate, was full to overflowing."

So much about the discharge of obligations for military defence carrying with it the right of self-government. The Indians have no desire to shirk their responsibility for the military defence of India; nor do they want to balk their contribution to the Imperial defence. Their demands in this respect may be thus summarised:

(1) That the Indian Army should be mainly officered by the Indians.

(2) That as much as is possible of the arms and ammunition equipment, and the military stores required for the Indian army be produced in India.

(3) That the strength of the British element be considerably reduced.

(4) That the nature of the Indian army, which is at present one of hired soldiers, be converted into that of a National Militia with a small standing army and a great reserve.

(5) That in order to do it, some kind of compulsory military training be introduced. All young men between the ages of 17 and 21 may be required to undergo military training and put in at least one year of military service.

(6) That as a preliminary step towards it the existing Arms Act be repealed and, under proper safeguards, the people be allowed to carry and possess arms in peace and war, so as to be familiar with their use.

(7) That slowly and gradually, as funds can be

> spared from the other demands more urgent and pressing, an Indian Navy be built.

Having explained the position of the Indian Nationalist in this matter, we will now see what Mr. Montagu and Lord Chelmsford say on this matter in their report. In Paragraph 328 they state the "Indian wishes" and point out that "for some years Indian politicians have been urging the right of Indians in general to bear arms in defence of their country"; and that "we have everywhere met a general demand from the political leaders for extended opportunities for military service," but that the subject being more or less outside the scope of their enquiry and "requirements of the future" being dependent "on the form of peace which is attained," they "leave this question for consideration hereafter with the note that it must be faced and settled."

In Paragraph 330 they deal with the question of "British Commissions for Indians."

"The announcement of his Majesty's Government that 'the bar which has hitherto prevented the admission of Indians to commissioned rank in His Majesty's Army should be removed' has established the principle that the Indian soldier can earn the King's commission by his military conduct. It is not enough merely to assert a principle. We must act on it. The services of the Indian army in the war and the great increase in its numbers make it necessary that a considerable number of commissions should now be given. The appointments made so far have been few. Other methods of appointment have not yet been decided on, but we are impressed with the necessity of grappling with the problem. We also wish to establish the principle that if an Indian is enlisted as a private in a

British unit of His Majesty's Army its commissioned ranks also should be open to him."

The "other methods of appointment" that have been announced since the report was signed are far from satisfactory. It has been said that the responsibility for this niggardly policy in the matter of admitting Indians to the Commissioned ranks of the army rests with the Home Government and that the Indian Government's recommendations were much more liberal. Now, as practical men, we fully realize that for some time to come, at least until British suspicion of India's desire to get out of the Empire is completely removed by the grant of responsible government to India, India's military policy and the Indian army must be controlled by the British executive. On that point all the parties in India are agreed. But it is absolutely necessary that some steps be at once taken to remove the stigma of military helplessness from India's forehead. Let the British retain the control and the command, but let us share the responsibility to some extent and let our young men be trained for the future defence of their Motherland. To deprive them of all means of doing that, to charge them with neglect of that paramount duty and then to urge it as a disqualification of civil liberties, is hardly fair.

VIII

THE EUROPEAN COMUNITY IN INDIA

> The old world, at least, believed in ideals. It believed that justice, fair play, liberty, righteousness must triumph in the end; that is, however you interpret the phrase, the old world believed in God, and it staked its existence on that belief. Millions of gallant young men volunteered to die for that divine faith. But if wrong emerged triumphant out of this conflict, the new world would feel in its soul that brute force alone counted in the government of man; and the hopelessness of the dark ages would once more fall on the earth like a cloud.
>
> DAVID LLOYD GEORGE
>
> "No Halfway House." Speech delivered at Gray's Inn, December 14, 1917.

A WHOLE section of the Report has been devoted to a consideration of the claims of the European Community in India. It is said:

"We cannot conclude without taking into due account the presence of a considerable community of non-official Europeans in India. In the main they are engaged in commercial enterprises; but besides these are the missions, European and American, which in furthering education, building up character, and inculcating healthier domestic habits have done work for which India should be grateful. There are also an appreciable number of retired officers and others whose working life has been given to India, settled in the cooler parts of the country. When complaints are rife that European commercial interests are selfish and drain the country of wealth which it ought to retain, it *is well to remind ourselves how much of India's material prosperity is due to European commerce.*" [The italics are ours].

We have no desire to raise a controversy over the assumption which underlies the last statement in the above extract. The authors are themselves cognizant of it when they remark, later on, that the "benefit" which India has received by her commercial development in European hands is "not less because it was incidental and not the purpose of the undertaking." These are matters on which the Indian Nationalist may well hold his own opinion and yet endorse the spirit of the following observations:

"Clearly it is the duty of British Commerce in India to identify itself with the interests of India, which are higher than the interests of any community; to take part in political life; to use its considerable wealth and opportunities to commend itself to India; and having demonstrated both its value and its good intentions, to be content to rest like other industries on the new foundation of Government in the wishes of the people. No less is it the wish of Indian politicians to respect the expectations which have been implicitly held out; to remember how India has profited by commercial development which only British capital and enterprise achieved; to bethink themselves that though the capital invested in private enterprises was not borrowed under any assurance that the existing form of government would endure, yet the favourable terms on which money was obtained for India's development were undoubtedly affected by the fact of British rule; and to abstain from advocating differential treatment aimed not so much at promoting Indian as at injuring British commerce."

We must say that the last insinuation is perfectly gratuitous. Nor is it correct to say even by implication that the non-official European community has hitherto abstained from taking part in politics. The fact is that Indian politics have hitherto been too greatly dominated by the British merchant both at home and in India. The British merchant doing business in India had to submit to the prior claims of the British manufacturers in Great Britain in matters in which their interests did not coincide, but otherwise their interests received the greatest possible attention from the Government of India. In proportion to their incomes derived from India by the employment of Indian labour on terms more or less guaranteed to them by the Indian Government's special legislation they have made the smallest possible contribution to the Indian Revenues; yet they have been the greatest possible hindrance in the development of Indian liberties. They have all the time owned a powerful press which has employed all the resources of education and enlightenment, all the powers of manipulating facts and figures in maintaining and strengthening the rule of autocracy in the country. We do not propose to open these wounds. But we cannot help remarking that so far they have exercised quite a disproportionate influence in the decisions of the Government of India. Those of them who are domiciled in the country are our brothers and no Indian has the least desire to do anything that will harm them in any way. Their importance must, in future, be determined not by their race or colour or creed but by their numbers, their education and their position in the economic life of the country. They must no longer lord it over the Indians simply because they are of European descent. They should claim no preferences or exemptions because of that fact. As an integral part of the Indian body politic they are entitled to all the consideration which they deserve by virtue of their intellectual or economic position. They should henceforth be Indo-British both in spirit and in name. They will find the Indians quite ready to forget the past and embrace them as brothers for the common prosperity of their joint country.

As regards the other European merchants who are not domiciled in India but are there just to make money and return to spend it in their native land, they are no more entitled to any place in the political machinery of the Indian Government than the Hindus who trade in the United States or in England. So far every European, of whatever nationality he might be, has occupied a position of privilege in India. He was granted rights which were denied to the sons of the soil. Every German or Austrian or Bulgarian could keep or carry any number and kind of arms he wanted without any license, while the natives of India, even of the highest position, could not do so unless exempted either by virtue of their rank or by the favour of the Administration. Jews and Armenians, Turks and Russians, Scandinavians, Danes, Italians and Swiss all enjoyed the privilege. When charged with any serious offence punishable by imprisonment for more than six months, they could claim trial by a jury having a majority of Europeans on it, while no Indian outside the Presidency towns of Bombay, Calcutta and Madras had that right. Even there, the jury trying an Indian could include a majority of Europeans. In the famous trial of Mr. B. G. Tilak in 1908, the jury was composed of seven Europeans and two Parsees. It is obvious that these discriminations in favour of the Europeans must cease and that no European not domiciled in India should enjoy a position of special privilege. Indians are noted for their hospitality and chivalry. Their own codes of honor effectively prevent them from doing any harm or injury to a foreigner. Every European doing business in India or on any other errand is a guest of honor and entitled to that treatment, provided he does not assume racial superiority and look down upon the people of the country and take advantage of their being subjects of a European power. No Indian will be so foolish as to injure the commercial development of his country by scaring the foreign trader or the foreign capitalist. All that he wants is freedom to lay down the terms on which that trade will be carried on consistently with the interests of India's millions. What he stands for is equality and reciprocity. As other peoples are free to name the conditions on which the foreign trader may do business in their countries, so must the Indians be. Nothing more and nothing less than this is demanded.

As regards the citizens of the British Empire also, the same right of reciprocity is demanded. We are glad that the representatives of the Dominions have recognized the justice of that claim and expressed their willingness to concede it.

Coming to the Missions, European and American, the advice given is rather gratuitous. The Indians have left nothing undone to show their gratitude to them for the good work done by them in spite of the fact that they, too, in the past, have not hesitated to use the fact of their race and colour for the benefit of their propaganda. The person of a religious man is sacred in the eyes of an Indian, regardless of his particular creed. The Christian missionary has so far enjoyed a unique position of safety and freedom in the country even to a greater extent than the Hindu or the Moslem priest. The latter have often quarrelled amongst themselves, but the former they have always respected and honored. There is absolutely no reason to think that this is likely to change in any way by the grant of political liberty to the Indians.

It is possible, however, that, with the growth of free thought in India, religious teachers of all denominations may not continue to be the recipients of the same honour as has been paid to them in the past by virtue of their religious office. Dogmatic religion, whether it be Hinduism, Mohammedanism or Christianity is in a state of decay. In that respect India is feeling the reaction of world forces and no amount of political coercion or repression can stop it. In my humble judgment the average Indian has thus far been more tolerant of and more considerate to the Christian missionary than the latter has been to the Indian. Even in the matter of gratitude the Christian missionary may with advantage learn from the Hindu. The instances are not rare in which all the hospitality, respect and honor which a Christian missionary has received during his stay in India have been repaid by the latter's freely traducing the character of the Indians in his home land. To no small degree is the Christian missionary responsible for the feeling of contempt with which the Indian is looked down upon in America and other countries of the West. We do not object to his speaking the truth, but it is not the truth that he always speaks. Of gratitude, at least, he gives no evidence.

The European Community in India is divided into two classes: (a) pure Europeans, who number a little less than 200,000 in the total population of 315,000,000. (178,908 in the British provinces and 20,868 in the native States.)

(b) Anglo-Indians, hitherto called Eurasians, who number about 83,000 (68,612 in British territories and 15,045 in the Native States). Thus the whole European community in India is less than 300,000.

IX

THE NATIVE STATES

THE Native States of India constitute one of the anomalies of Indian political life. They are the honored remnants of the old order of things — an order in which personal bravery, resourcefulness and leadership with or without capacity for successful intrigue enabled individuals to carve out kingdoms and principalities for themselves and their legal successors.

In the case of some of these Native States the genealogies of the ruling houses go back to the early centuries of the Christian era by historical evidence and to pre-Christian times by tradition. Their origin is somewhat shrouded in mystery. In popular belief they are the descendants of gods — gods of light and life, the Sun and the Moon. Next to the Royal family of Japan, they are perhaps the only houses among the rulers of the earth which can claim such an ancient and unbroken lineage of royalty with sovereignty of one kind or another always vested in them. There have been times in their history when the royal heads of these states had no house to live in and no bed to sleep on, much less a territory to rule and an army to command. This was, however, a part of their royalty. In struggles against powerful enemies, sometimes of their own race and religion, but more often foreign aggressors of different blood and creed, they were many a time worsted and driven to extreme straits of poverty and helplessness. In peace or in war, in prosperity or in misery, they never gave up the struggle. Their right to lead their people and to rule their country they never yielded for a moment. It is true that sometimes they submitted to the superior power of the enemy and accepted a position of subordination, though in one case, at least, even this was done only for a short time under the Moguls. In the darker days of Indian history, when the military devastation of foreign invaders left nothing but tears and blood, ruin and ashes, defeat and misery in their track, these houses kept the lamp of hope burning. For full ten centuries they carried on a struggle of life and death, sometimes momentarily succumbing before the overwhelming force of their adversaries, but only to rise again in fresh vigor and life to reclaim their heritage and preserve their own and their country's independence.

The *Sessodias* of Mewar called the *Ranas* of Mewar (Udaipur) and the Rahtores of Marwar (including Jodhpur, Bikaner, Rutlam, Kishangarh and Alwar) have written many a glorious page of Mediaeval Indian history and dyed it with their own blood as well as that of their adversaries. Not only their men but their women have made themselves immortal by their bravery, chivalry, purity and self-immolation. The one thing which distinguishes the Indian Rajput from the peoples of other lands is that he has never waged war against the poor, the helpless and the defenceless. Numberless men gave their lives freely and ungrudgingly not only in protecting the lives of their own women and children but also in doing the same service to the women and children of their enemies. The Rajput never fought an unfair fight. He never took advantage of the helplessness of his enemy and always gave him right of way and the use of his best weapons for a free and fair fight in the open. Anyone desirous of knowing their deeds may read them in that poem in prose, known as the Annals of Rajhasthan by Col. Todd. Col. Todd has drawn a most faithful and thrilling picture of Rajput bravery and Rajput chivalry in a language worthy of the best traditions of English literature. Here and there in matters of minor details his authority has been questioned; otherwise the results of his monumental labors still remain the best picture of Rajput India. The Rajput States of India are thus the objects of reverent honor to the 220 million Hindus of that country. Next to the Rajput States comes the native ruling family of Mysore as the representative of a very ancient Hindu Kingdom. The Mahratta States are the remnants of the Mahratta Empire and the Sikhs those of the Sikh Commonwealth. The biggest of all the Indian Native States, Hyderabad, arose out of the ruins of the Mogul Empire and is supposed to be the most powerful guardian of Moslem culture and tradition. From this description the reader will at once see why the Native States are so dear to the peoples of India and why the Indian educated party has always stood by the Native States, whenever either their treaty rights or the personal dignity and status of their chiefs was threatened by the British authorities. Lord Dalhousie's policy of annexation by lapse was so much resented by the people of India that it had almost cost the British their Indian Empire. Only in the Native States do the Indians see remaining traces of their former independence. That fact alone covers all the defects of native rule or misrule in the States, in their eyes. Some of these Native States have been so well administered that in education, social reform and industrial advancement they are far ahead of the neighboring British territories. But their chief merit lies in the fact that ordinarily the people get enough food to eat and are seemingly happier than British subjects. This fact has been noticed by several competent observers of contemporary Indian life, among them the Right Honorable Mr. Fisher, President of the Board of Education in England. In his book *The Empire and the Future* he has observed:

"My impression is that the inhabitants of a well governed native state are on the whole happier and more contented than the inhabitants of British India. *They are more lightly taxed;* the pace of the administration is less urgent and exacting; their sentiment is gratified by the splendor of a native court and by the dominion of an Indian government. They feel that they do things for themselves instead of having everything done for them by a cold and alien benevolence." (Italics are ours)

But after all that is favourable to the Native States of India has been said, their existence in their present form remains a political anomaly. As at present situated, they are an effective hindrance to complete Indian unity. Although "India is in fact as well as by legal definition, one geographical whole," yet these Native States, occupying about one-third of the total area of the country and with a population of about 70 million will, for a long time, prevent its becoming a homogeneous political whole. Thus a circumstance which was hitherto looked upon as a piece of good luck will operate as a misfortune.

"The Native States of India are about 700 in number. They embrace the widest variety of country and jurisdiction. They vary in size from petty States like Rewa, in Rajputana, with an area of 19 square miles, and the Simla Hill States, which are little more than small holdings, to States like Hyderabad, as large as Italy, with a population of thirteen millions." [1]

The general position as regards the rights and obligations of the Native States has been thus summed up by the distinguished authors of the joint Report (Lord Chelmsford and Mr. Montagu):

"The States are guaranteed security from without; the paramount power acts for them in relation to foreign powers and other States, and it intervenes when the internal peace of their territories is seriously threatened. On the other hand the States' relations to foreign powers are those of the paramount power; they share the obligation for the common defence; and they are under a general responsibility for the good government and welfare of their territories."

As regards the assimilation of the principles of modern life, it is remarked in the same document:

"Many of them have adopted our civil and criminal codes. Some have imitated and even further extended our educational system. . . . They have not all been equally able to assimilate new principles. They are in all stages of development, patriarchal, feudal or more advanced, while in a few states are found the beginnings of representative institutions. The characteristic features of all of them, however, including

[1] The *Indian Year Book* for 1918, p. 81.

the most advanced, are the personal rule of the Prince and his control over legislation and the administration of justice."

Under the circumstances the question of questions is how these territories are going to fall into line with the British controlled area in the matter of the development of responsible Government. We will once more quote the opinion of the Secretary of State for India and the Viceroy, who say:

"We know that the States cannot be unaffected by constitutional development in adjoining provinces. Some of the more enlightened and thoughtful of the Princes, among whom are included some of the best known names, have realised this truth, and have themselves raised the question of their own share in any scheme of reform. Others of the Princes — again including some of the most honored names — desire only to leave matters as they are. We feel the need for caution in this matter. It would be a strange reward for loyalty and devotion to force new ideas upon those who did not desire them; but it would be no less strange, if out of consideration for those who perhaps represent gradually vanishing ideas, we were to refuse to consider the suggestions of others who have been no less loyal and devoted. Looking ahead to the future we can picture India to ourselves only as presenting the external semblance to some form of 'federation.' The provinces will ultimately become self-governing units, held together by the central Government which will deal solely with matters of common concern to all of them. But the matters common to the British provinces are also to a great extent those in which the Native States are interested — defence, tariffs, exchange, opium, salt, railways and posts and telegraphs. The gradual concentration of the Government of India upon such matters will therefore make it easier for the States, while retaining the autonomy which they cherish in internal matters, to enter into closer association with the central Government if they wish to do so. But though we have no hesitation in forecasting such a development as possible, the last thing that we desire is to attempt to force the pace. Influences are at work which need no artificial stimulation. All that we need or can do is to open the door to the natural developments of the future."

In Paragraphs 302 to 305 the authors of the Report state the process by which this development may be expedited. Disavowing any intention of forcibly altering treaty rights, they propose to classify the States into (*a*) those that have "full authority over their internal affairs," (*b*) those "in which Government exercises through its Agents large powers of internal control," (*c*) those who are really no more "than mere owners of a few acres of land." It is further pointed out that hitherto the

"general clause which occurs in many of the treaties to the effect that the Chief shall remain absolute Ruler of his country has not in the past precluded and does not even now preclude 'interference with the administration by Government through the agency of its representatives at the Native Courts.' We need hardly say that such interference has not been employed in wanton disregard of treaty obligations. During the earlier days of our intimate relations with the States British agents found themselves compelled, often against their will, to assume responsibility for the welfare of the people, to restore order out of chaos, to prevent inhuman practices, and to guide the hands of a weak or incompetent Ruler as the only alternative to the termination of his rule. So too, at the present day, the Government of India acknowledges as trustee, a responsibility (which the Princes themselves desire to maintain) for the proper administration of States during a minority, and also an obligation for the prevention or correction of flagrant misgovernment."

And also that:

"the position hitherto taken up by Government has been that the conditions under which some of the treaties were executed have undergone material changes, and the literal fulfilment of particular obligations which they impose has become impracticable. Practice has been based on the theory that treaties must be read as a whole, and that they must be interpreted in the light of the relation established between the parties not only at the time when a particular treaty was made, but subsequently."

On these grounds it is proposed to establish a Council of Princes to which questions which affect the States generally or are of concern to the Empire as a whole, or to British India and the States in common, may be referred for advice and opinion. So long as the Princes do not intervene either formally or informally in the internal affairs of British India, we have no objection to the scheme. On the other hand, we do hope some method will be found by which, with the consent of the parties interested the smaller principalities scattered all over the country may, for administrative purposes, be merged either in the British area or in the bigger Native States which possess full power of autonomy over their internal affairs. In the long run it will be comparatively easy to convert the latter to an acceptance of the modern principles of government if the number of Native States is reduced and their people achieve that solidarity which comes by community of interests and ideas. In this connection it is a happy augury for the future that some of the highest Chiefs like those of Mysore, Baroda, Gwaliar, Indore, Kashmir, Bikaner, Jodhpore, Alwar, and Patiala are alive to the importance of marching with the times. The people of British India owe them a great debt of gratitude for the moral support they have given to their claim for responsible Government by coming out openly and freely in favour of the proposed advance. We are sure that these Princes will in due time take measures to bring their own territories in line with the British provinces and thus strengthen the ties that bind them to their own peoples as well as to the other people of India. After all, there can be no manner of doubt, as the authors of the report predict,

"that the processes at work in British India cannot leave the States untouched and must in time affect even those whose ideas and institutions are of the most conservative and feudal character."

It is the path of wisdom and sagacity to recognise the world forces that are at work. No amount of ancient prestige can prevent the people from coming into their own. The age of despotism is gone and the autocrats of today must sooner or later hand over their powers to the people. The more they conciliate them the longer perhaps they may be able to lead them. They may continue as leaders for a long time, but as autocratic dispensers of favours and fortunes they cannot remain, perhaps not even for their life time.

In our judgment this part of the Montagu-Chelmsford Report is no less important for the future of Indian democracy than the others that directly deal with

British India, and we hope that whatever might be the policy as regards the existing States the new law will make it impossible for the Government of India and the Secretary of State to create any new States in the future. It is monstrous to transfer millions of human beings from one kind of political rule to another like so many cattle, as was done in 1911. The present rule of any Indian Maharaja may be as good or as bad as that of a British Governor or Lieutenant Governor, but the latter has in it greater democratic potentialities than the former, for the mere fact, if for no other, that, while the British are more or less amenable to world opinion, the rulers of Native States are not. It is inhuman, and not in accord with modern ideas of right and wrong to reward somebody's loyalty by giving him power of life and death over numerous fellow beings, otherwise than in due course of law. Even the mighty British Government is not the owner of the bodies and souls of its subjects in India. How, then, can it assume the right of abandoning them to the absolute rule of a single individual, however worthy or loyal he may be? We hope this stupid way of rewarding loyal services may be ended by an express provision to that effect in the statute which will be passed relating to the reorganization of the Government of India.

In this connection the following observations made in a leading editorial of the *Servant of India*, Poona (February 16, 1919), are worthy of attention:

"A hundred years ago, it was decidedly in the interests of British rule, and probably also in the interests of the people of India generally, that the small, ill-governed, and eternally fighting states of India should come under the suzerainty of a single powerful power. It may be regarded as a historical misfortune that this power happened then to be foreign, though many regard this contact with a virile civilization as the making of India. This suzerainty could then be established duly by entering into treaties with these states and guaranteeing them certain rights and privileges. But these treaties have now assumed in the eyes of the descendants of the original princes an air of inspiration; they have become a kind of perpetuity. They always come in the way of any improvement. When any new policy is proposed to them, they are always prepared to say, 'This is not in the bond.' One may be allowed to speculate as to how many of these Highnesses would have survived to this day to put forward this claim in the absence of the suzerain power. Thrones in ancient days were as unstable as they are becoming now in Europe. It is hardly possible that the present popular wave in Europe would not have touched our Native States. The subjects of the states would have clamoured for a recognition of their rights, and they would have had their way. But now the princes feel quite secure. Have they not got their treaties? As a result there is no political life at all in the Native States. The most ardent advocate of Home Rule would be most violently against migration to a Native State. The real problem of the Native States is how to get over the treaties when they conflict with the interests of their subjects. The questions discussed at the Chiefs' Conference leave us comparatively cold, as they entirely neglect the people most concerned. The questions of the rights of the chiefs and their salutes or precedence are in our opinion of a very secondary importance. A renowned statesman in Europe gave at the utmost a life of a dozen years to the most solemn treaty between two countries, for in that period circumstances alter and the solid foundation for the treaty cracks. Is it not high time that the treaties with the chiefs should be revised after over a hundred years? It would indeed redound to their credit if the chiefs themselves come forward to submit to such readjustment. Perhaps their autocratic and irresponsible power may have to suffer some diminution. But if they consent to that diminution so as to give it to their subjects in the modern democratic spirit, the real power and influence of the Native States will increase incalculably. It is in this direction we wish to see a solution of the problem of the Native States which are nowadays working as a brake on our national progress."

X

THE PROPOSALS

> There are epochs in the history of the world when in a few raging years the character, the destiny, of the whole race is determined for unknown ages. This is one.
>
> DAVID LLOYD GEORGE
>
> "Sowing the Winter Wheat." Speech delivered at Carnarvon, to a meeting of constituents, after becoming Prime Minister, February 3, 1917.

PART II of the Report contains the scheme which Mr. Montagu and Lord Chelmsford propose for the solution of the problem which they had set themselves to solve in Part I. In giving their reasons for a new policy they observe:

"*No further development* (*on old lines*) *is possible unless we are going to give the people of India some responsibility for their own government.* But no one can imagine that no further development is necessary. *It is evident that the present machinery of government no longer meets the needs of the time; it works slowly and it produces irritation;* there is a widespread demand on the part of educated Indian opinion for its alteration; and the need for advance is recognised by official opinion also." [Italics are ours.]

The new policy sketched by them is, in their judgment, "the logical outcome of the past. Indians must be enabled, in so far as they attain responsibility, to determine for themselves what they want done

". . . such limitations on powers as we are now proposing are due only to the obvious fact that time is necessary in order to train both representatives and electorates for the work which we desire them to undertake; and that we offer Indians opportunities at short intervals to prove the progress they are making and to make good their claim, not by the method of agitation but by positive demonstration, to the further stages in self-government which we have just indicated."

That is the only basis on which they maintain they can hope to see in India "the growth of a conscious feeling of organic unity with the Empire as a whole." With these and a few more prefatory remarks about the educational problem and the attitude of the ryot and the enunciation of the general principles on which their proposals are based they proceed to formulate their scheme, starting first with the provinces.

I

The proposals relating to Provincial Government may be noticed under the following heads:

(*a*) *Financial devolution:* It is proposed that henceforth there should be a complete separation of the provincial finances from those of the Government of India; that, reserving certain sources of revenue for the Government of India, all others should be made over to the Provincial Governments with the proviso that the first charge on all Provincial revenues will be a contribution towards the maintenance of the Government of India, considered necessary and demanded by the latter. A certain amount of power to impose fresh taxes and to raise loans is also conceded to the provincial Governments subject to the veto of the Government of India.

(*b*) *Legislative devolution:* "It is our intention," say the authors of the report, "to reserve to the Government of India a general overriding power of legislation for the discharge of all functions which it will have to perform. It should be enabled under this power to intervene in any province for the protection and enforcement of the interests for which it is responsible; to legislate on any provincial matter in respect of which uniformity of legislation is desirable, either for the whole of India or for any two or more provinces; and to pass legislation which may be adopted either *simpliciter* or with modifications by any province which may wish to make use of it. We think that the Government of India must be the sole judge of the propriety of any legislation which it may undertake under any one of these categories, and that its competence so to legislate should not be open to challenge in the courts. Subject to these reservations we intend that within the field which may be marked off for provincial legislative control the sole legislative power shall rest with the provincial legislatures." It is not proposed to put a statutory limitation on the power of the Government of India to legislate for the provinces, but it is hoped that "constitutional practice" will prevent the central Government interfering in provincial matters unless the interests for which the latter is responsible are directly affected.

(*c*) *Provincial Executive:* Article 220 gives the Governor the power to appoint "one or two additional members of his Government as members without portfolio for purposes of consultation and advice."

These, in substance, are the proposals of the Secretary of State and the Government of India for the future government of the provinces into which India is divided. Some of these latter and some other tracts are expressly excluded from the operation of these recommendations. It will be at once observed that this is neither autonomy nor home rule. It is a kind of hybrid system with final powers of veto and control vested in the Government of India. The provision as to Provincial Legislatures make it still more complicated.

"Let us now explain how we contemplate in future that the executive Governments of the provinces shall be constituted. As we have seen, three provinces are now governed by a Governor and an Executive Council of three members, of whom one is in practice an Indian and two are usually appointed from the Indian Civil Service, although the law says only that they must be qualified by twelve years' service under the Crown in India. One province, Bihar and Orissa, is administered by a Lieutenant-Governor with a council of three constituted in the same way. The remaining five provinces, that is to say, the three Lieutenant-Governorships of the United Provinces, the Punjab and Burma and the Chief Commissionerships of the Central Provinces and Assam are under the administration of a single official Head. We find throughout India a very general desire for the extension of Council government. . . . Our first proposition, therefore, is that in all these provinces singleheaded administration must cease and be replaced by collective administration.

"In determining the structure of the Executive we have to bear in mind the duties with which it will be charged. We start with the two postulates; the complete responsibility for the government cannot be given immediately without inviting a breakdown, and that some responsibility must be given at once if our scheme is to have any value. We have defined responsibility as consisting primarily in amenability to constituents, and in the second place in amenability to an assembly. We do not believe that there is any way of satisfying these governing conditions other than by making a division of the functions of the Government, between those which may be made over to popular control and those which for the present must remain in official hands. . . . We may call these the 'reserved' and 'transferred' subjects respectively. It then follows that for the management of these two categories there must be some form of executive body, with a legislative organ in harmony with it. . . .

. . . .

"We propose therefore that in each province the executive Government should consist of two parts. One part would comprise the head of the province and an executive council of two members. In all provinces the head of the Government would be known as Governor. . . . One of the two Executive Councillors would in practice be a European qualified by long official experience, and the other would be an Indian. It has been urged that the latter should be an elected member of the provincial legislative council. It is unreasonable that choice should be so limited. It should be open to the Governor to recommend whom he wishes. . . . The Governor in council would have charge of the reserved subjects. The other part of the government would consist of one member or more than one member, according to the number and importance of the transferred subjects, chosen by the Governor from the elected members of the Legislative council. They would be known as ministers. They would be members of the executive

Government but not members of the Executive Council; they would be appointed for the life-time of the legislative council, and if reelected to that body would be re-eligible for appointment as members of the Executive. As we have said, they would not hold office at the will of the legislature but at that of their constituents.

"The portfolios dealing with the transferred subjects would be committed to the ministers, and on these subjects the ministers together with the Governor would form the administration. On such subjects their decision would be final, subject only to the Governor's advice and control. We do not contemplate that from the outset the Governor should occupy the position of a purely constitutional Governor who is bound to accept the decisions of his ministers."

(*d*) *Provincial Legislatures:* "We propose there shall be in each province an enlarged legislative council, differing in size and composition from province to province, with a substantial elected majority, elected by direct election on a broad franchise, with such communal and special representation as may be necessary."

The questions of franchise and special and communal representation have been entrusted to a special committee the report of which is shortly expected. The same committee will also decide how many official members there will be on each Legislative Council. It is provided that the Governor shall be the President of the Council and will have the power to nominate a Vice-president from the official members. As to the effect of resolutions it is said that "we do not propose that resolutions, whether on reserved or transferred subjects should be binding."

The classification of the reserved and transferred

subjects was also left to a special committee which has since concluded its labours and whose report is awaited with interest.

Legislation on reserved subjects:

"For the purpose of enabling the provincial Government to get through its legislation on reserved subjects, we propose that the head of the Government should have power to certify that a Bill dealing with a reserved subject is a measure 'essential to the discharge of his responsibility for the peace or tranquillity of the province or of any part thereof, or for the discharge of his responsibility for the reserved subjects.' . . . The Bill will be read and its general principles discussed in the full legislative council. It will at this stage be open to the council by a majority vote to request the Governor to refer to the Government of India, whose decision on the point shall be final, on the question whether the certified Bill deals with a reserved subject. If no such reference is made, or if the Government of India decide that the certificate has been properly given, the Bill will then be automatically referred to a Grand Committee of the council. Its composition should reproduce as nearly as possible the proportion of the various elements in the larger body. . . . the grand committee in every council should be constituted so as to comprise from 40 to 50 per cent. of its strength. It should be chosen for each Bill, partly by election by ballot, and partly by nomination. The Governor should have power to nominate a bare majority exclusive of himself. Of the members so nominated not more than two-thirds should be officials, and the elected element should be elected *ad hoc* by the elected members of the council on the system of the transferable vote."

"On reference to the grand committee, the Bill will be debated by that body in the ordinary course, if necessary referred to a select committee, to which body we think that the grand committee should have power to appoint any member of the legislative council whether a member of the grand committee or not. The select committee will, as at present, have power to take evidence. Then, after being debated in the grand committee and modified as may be determined, the Bill will be reported to the whole council. The council will have the right to discuss the Bill again generally, but will not be able to reject it, or to amend it except on the motion of a member of the executive council. The Governor will then appoint a time limit within which the Bill may be debated in the council, and on its expiry it will pass automatically. But during such discussion the council will have the right to pass a resolution recording any objection which refers to the principle or details of the measure (but not, of course, to the certificate of its character), and any such resolution will accompany the Act when, after being signed by the Governor, it is submitted to the Governor General and the Secretary of State."

Provincial Budget: . . . the provincial budget should be framed by the executive Government as a whole. The first charge on provincial revenues will be the contribution to the Government of India; and after that the supply for the reserved subjects will have priority. The allocation of supply for the transferred subjects will be decided by the ministers. If the revenue is insufficient for their needs, the question of new taxation will be decided by the Governor and the ministers. We are bound to recognise that in time new taxation will be necessary, for no conceivable economies can finance the new developments which are to be anticipated. The budget will then be laid before the council which will discuss it and vote by resolution upon the allotments. If the legislative council rejects or modifies the proposed allotment for reserved subjects, the Governor should have power to insist on the whole or any part of the allotment originally provided, if for reasons to be stated he certifies its necessity in the terms which we have already suggested. We are emphatically of opinion that the Governor in Council must be empowered to obtain the supply which he declares to be necessary for the discharge of his responsibilities. Except in so far as the Governor exercises this power the budget would be altered in accordance with the resolutions carried in council."

Modification of the Scheme by the Government of India. "After five years' time from the first meeting of the reformed councils we suggest that the Government of India should hear applications from either the provincial Government or the provincial council for the modification of the reserved and transferred lists of the province; and that, after considering the evidence laid before them, they should recommend for the approval of the Secretary of State the transfer of such further subjects to the transferred list as they think desirable. On the other hand, if it should be made plain to them that certain functions have been seriously maladministered, it will be open to them, with the sanction of the Secretary of State, to retransfer subjects from the transferred to the reserved list, or to place restrictions for the future on the minister's powers in respect of certain transferred subjects. . . . But it is also desirable to complete the responsibility of the ministers for the transferred subjects. This should come in one of two ways, either at the initiative of the council if it desires and is prepared to exercise greater control over the ministers, or at the discretion of the Government of India, which may wish to make this change as a condition of the grant of new, or of the maintainance of existing, powers. We propose, therefore, that the Government of India may, when hearing such applications, direct that the ministers' salaries, instead of any longer being treated as a reserved subject, and, therefore, protected in the last resort by the Governor's order from interference should be specifically voted each year by the legislative council;

or, failing such direction by the Government of India, it should be open to the councils at that time or subsequently to demand by resolution that such ministers' salaries should be so voted, and the Government of India should thereupon give effect to such request."

Periodic commissions: . . . Ten years after the first meeting of the new councils established under the Statute a commission should be appointed to review the position. Criticism has been expressed in the past of the composition of Royal Commissions, and it is our intention that the commission which we suggest should be regarded as authoritative and should derive its authority from Parliament itself. The names of the commissioners, therefore, should be submitted by the Secretary of State to both Houses of Parliament for approval by resolution. The commissioners' mandate should be to consider whether by the end of the term of the legislature then in existence it would be possible to establish complete responsible government in any province or provinces, or how far it would be possible to approximate it in others; to advise on the continued reservation of any departments for the transfer of which to popular control it has been proved to their satisfaction that the time had not yet come; to recommend the retransfer of other matters to the control of the Governor in Council if serious maladministration were established; and to make any recommendations for the working of responsible government or the improvement of the constitutional machinery which experience of the systems in operation may show to be desirable. . . .

"There are several other important matters, germane in greater or less degree to our main purpose, which the commission should review. They should investigate the progress made in admitting Indians into the higher ranks of the public service. They should examine the apportionment of the financial burden of India with a view to adjusting it more fairly between the provinces. The commission should also examine the development of education among the people and the progress and working of local self-governing bodies. Lastly the commission should consider the working of the franchise and the constitution of electorates, including the important matter of the retention of communal representation. Indeed, we regard the development of a broad franchise as the arch on which the edifice of self-government must be raised; for we have no intention that our reforms should result merely in the transfer of powers from a bureaucracy to an oligarchy. . . ."

"In proposing the appointment of a commission ten years after the new Act takes effect we wish to guard against possible misunderstanding. We would not be taken as implying that there can be established by that time complete responsible government in the provinces. In many of the provinces no such consummation can follow in the time named. The pace will be everywhere unequal, though progress in one province will always stimulate progress elsewhere; but undue expectations might be aroused, if we indicated any opinion as to the degree of approximation to complete self-government that might be reached even in one or two of the most advanced provinces. The reasons that make complete responsibility at present impossible are likely to continue operative in some degree even after a decade."

II

The proposals regarding the Government of India called the Central Government may be thus summed up:

(a) *General:* "We have already made our opinion clear that pending the development of responsible government in the provinces the Government of India must remain responsible only to Parliament. In other words, in all matters which it judges to be essential to the discharge of its responsibilities for peace, order, and good government it must, saving only for its accountability to Parliament, retain indisputable power."

(b) *The Governor General's Executive Council:* "We would therefore abolish such statutory restrictions as now exist in respect of the appointment of Members of the Governor General's Council, so as to give greater elasticity both in respect to the size of the Government and the distribution of work."

At present there is one Indian member in the Viceroy's Executive Council consisting of six ordinary members and one extraordinary besides the Viceroy. This scheme recommends the appointment of another Indian.

(c) *The Indian Legislative Council.*

I. Legislative Assembly: "We recommend therefore that the strength of the legislative council, to be known in future as the Legislative Assembly of India, should be raised to a total strength of about 100 members, so as to be far more truly representative of British India. We propose that two-thirds of this total should be returned by election; and that one-third should be nominated by the Governor General, of which third not less than a third again should be non-officials selected with the object of representing minority or special interests. . . . Some special representation, we think, there must be, as for European and Indian commerce, and also for the large landlords. There should be also communal representation for Muhammadans in most provinces and also for Sikhs in the Punjab."

II. The Council of State: "We do not propose to institute a complete bi-cameral system, but to create a second chamber, known as the Council of State, which shall take its part in ordinary legislative business and shall be the final legislative authority in matters which the government regards as essential. The Council of State will be composed of 50 members, exclusive of the Governor General, who would be President, with power to appoint a Vice-President who would normally take his place: not more than 25 will be officials, including the members of the executive council, and 4 would be non-officials nominated by the Governor General. Official members would be eligible for nomination to both the Legislative Assembly and the Council of State. There would be 21 elected members of whom 15 will be returned by the non-official members of the provincial legislative councils, each council returning two members, other than those of Burma, the Central Provinces and Assam which will return one member each. . . .

"Inasmuch as the Council of State will be the supreme legislative authority for India on all crucial questions and also the revising authority upon all Indian legislation, we desire to attract to it the services of the best men available in the country. We desire that the Council of State should develop something of the experience and dignity of a body of Elder Statesmen; and we suggest therefore that the Governor General in Council should make regulations as to the qualification of candidates for election to that body which will ensure that their status and position and record of services will give to the Council a senatorial character, and the qualities usually regarded as appropriate to a revising chamber."

III. Legislative procedure: "Let us now explain how this legislative machinery will work. It will make for clearness to deal separately with Government Bills and Bills introduced by non-official members. A Government Bill will ordinarily be introduced and carried through all the usual stages in the Legislative Assembly. It will then go in the ordinary course to the Council of State, and if there amended in any way which the Assembly is not willing to accept, it will be submitted to a joint session of both Houses, by whose decision its ultimate fate will be decided. This will be the ordinary course of legislation. But it might well happen that amendments made by the Council of State were such as to be essential in the view of the Government if the purpose with which the Bill was originally introduced was to be achieved, and in this case the Governor General in Council would certify that the amendments were essential to the interests of peace, order, or good government. The assembly would then not have power to reject or modify these amendments, nor would they be open to revision in a joint session.

"We have to provide for two other possibilities. Cases may occur in which the Legislative Assembly refuses leave to the introduction of a Bill or throws out a Bill which the Government regarded as necessary. For such a contingency we would provide that if leave to introduce a Government Bill is refused, or if the Bill is thrown out at any stage, the Government should have the power, on the certificate of the Governor General in Council that the Bill is essential to the interests of peace, order, or good government, to refer it *de novo* to the Council of State; and if the Bill, after being taken in all its stages through the Council of State, was passed by that body, it would become law without further reference to the Assembly. Further, there may be cases when the consideration of a measure by both chambers would take too long if the emergency which called for the measure is to be met. Such a contingency should rarely arise; but we advise that in cases of emergency, so certified by the Governor General in Council, it should be open to the Government to introduce a Bill in the Council of State, and upon its being passed there merely to report it to the Assembly."

IV. Powers of dissolution, etc.: "The Governor General should in our opinion have power at any time to dissolve either the Legislative Assembly or the Council of State or both these bodies. It is perhaps unnecessary to add that the Governor General and the Secretary of State should retain their existing powers of assent, reservation, and disallowance to all Acts of the Indian legislature. The present powers of the Governor General in Council under section 71 of the Government of India Act. 1915, to make regulations proposed by local Governments for the peace and good government of backward tracts of territory should also be preserved; with the modification that it will in future rest with the Head of the province concerned to propose such regulations to the Government of India."

V. Fiscal legislation: "Fiscal legislation will, of course, be subject to the procedure which we have recommended in respect of Government Bills. The budget will be introduced in the Legislative Assembly but the Assembly will not vote it. Resolutions upon budget matters and upon all other questions, whether moved in the Assembly or in the Council of State, will continue to be advisory in character."

(d) Privy Council: "We have a further recommendation to make. We would ask that His Majesty may be graciously pleased to approve the institution of a Privy Council for India. . . . The Privy Council's office would be to advise the Governor General when he saw fit to consult it on questions of policy and administration."

(e) Periodic commissions: "At the end of the last chapter we recommended that ten years after the institution of our reforms, and again at intervals of twelve years thereafter, a commission approved by Parliament should investigate the working of the changes introduced into the provinces, and recommend as to their further progress. It should be equally the duty of the commission to examine and report upon the new constitution of the Government of India, with particular reference to the working of the machinery for representation, the procedure by certificate, and the results of joint sessions."

III

India Office in London

The principal proposals under this head may be thus summarized;

"We advise that the Secretary of State's salary, like that of all other Ministers of the Crown, should be defrayed from home revenues and voted annually by Parliament. This will enable any live questions of Indian administration to be discussed by the House of Commons in Committee of Supply. . . . It might be thought to follow that the whole charges of the India Office establishment should similarly be transferred to the home Exchequer; but this matter is complicated by a series of past transactions, and by the amount of agency work which the India Office does on behalf of the Government of India; and we advise that our proposed committee upon the India Office organization should examine it and taking these factors into consideration, determine which of the various India Office charges should be so transferred, and which can legitimately be retained as a burden on Indian revenues.

"But the transfer of charges which we propose, although it will give reality to the debates on Indian affairs, will not ensure in Parliament a better informed or a more sustained interest in India. We feel that this result can only be accomplished by appointing a Select Committee of Parliament on Indian affairs."

The above in substance is the proposed scheme. In India it has met with varied response. The European community does not approve of it. They think it is too radical. The European Services have struck a note of rebellion threatening to resign in case of its acceptance by Parliament. The Indian politicians are divided into two camps. Their views are best represented by the following tabular statement which we reproduce from the Indian newspapers.

A COMPARISON BETWEEN THE RESOLUTIONS RELATING TO THE REFORM PROPOSALS PASSED

Ordinary Rights of Citizens

By the Special Congress

Resolution IV. The Government of India shall have undivided administrative authority on matters directly concerning peace, tranquillity and defence of the country subject to the following:

That the Statute to be passed by Parliament should include the Declaration of the Rights of the people of India as British citizens:

(a) That all Indian subjects of his Majesty and all the subjects naturalized or resident in India are equal before the law, and there shall be no penal nor administrative law in force in the country whether substantive or procedural of a discriminative nature.

(b) That no Indian subject of his Majesty shall be liable to suffer in liberty, life, property or of association, free speech or in respect of writing, except under sentence by an ordinary Court of Justice, and as a result of a lawful and open trial.

(c) That every Indian subject shall be entitled to bear arms, subject to the purchase of a licence, as in Great Britain, and that the right shall not be taken away save by a sentence of an ordinary Court of Justice.

By the Moderate Conference

(V) This Conference urges that legislation of an exceptional character having the effect of curtailing ordinary rights such as the freedom of the press and public meetings and open judicial trial, should not be carried through the Council of State alone, or in spite of the declared opinion of the Legislative Assembly of India, except in a time of war or internal disturbance, without the approval of the Select Committee of the House of Commons proposed to be set up under the Scheme unless such legislation is of a temporary character and limited to a period of one year only, the said legislation being in any case made renewable without such approval in the last resort.

10

(c) All racial inequalities in respect of trial by jury, the rules made under the Arms Act, etc. should be removed and the latter should be so amended as to provide for the possession and carrying of arms by Indians under liberal conditions.

(d) A complete separation of judicial and executive functions of all district officers should be made, at least in all

(d) That the Press shall be free, and that no licence nor security shall be demanded on the registration of a press or a newspaper.

(e) That corporal punishment shall not be inflicted on any Indian serving in his Majesty's Army or Navy save under conditions applying equally to all other British subjects.

major provinces, at once, and the judiciary placed under the jurisdiction of the highest court of the province.

Fiscal Autonomy

Resolution V. This Congress is strongly of opinion that it is essential for the welfare of the Indian people that the Indian Legislature should have the same measure of fiscal autonomy which the self-governing dominions of the Empire possess.

(VI) Saving such equal and equitable Imperial obligations as may be agreed upon as resting on all parts of the Empire, the Government of India, acting under the control of the Legislature, should enjoy the same power of regulating the fiscal policy of India as the Governments of the self-governing dominions enjoy of regulating their fiscal policy.

Reform Proposals

Resolution VI. That this Congress appreciates the earnest attempt on the part of the Right Hon. the Secretary of State and his Excellency the Viceroy to inaugurate a system of responsible government in India, and, while it recognizes that some of the proposals constitute an advance on the present conditions in some directions, it is of opinion that the proposals are as a whole disappointing and unsatisfactory, and suggests the following modifications as absolutely necessary to constitute a substantial step towards responsible government:

(III) 'This Conference cordially welcomes the Reform Proposals of the Secretary of State and the Viceroy of India as constituting a distinct advance on present conditions as regards the Government of India and the Provincial Governments and also a real step towards the progressive realization of "responsible government" in the Provincial Government in due fulfillment of the terms of the announcement of August 20, 1917. As such this Conference accords its hearty support to those proposals, and, while suggesting necessary modifications and improvements therein, expresses its grateful appreciation of the earnest effort of Mr. Montagu and Lord Chelmsford to start the country on a career of genuine and lasting progress towards the promised goal.'

(V) 'This Conference regards all attempts at the condemnation or rejection of the Reform Scheme as a whole as ill advised, and in particular protests emphatically against the reactionary attitude assumed towards it by the Indo-British Association and some European public bodies in this country which is certain to produce, if successfully persisted in, an extremely undesirable state of feeling between England and India and imperil the cause of ordered progress in this country. This Conference, therefore, most earnestly urges his Majesty's Government and Parliament of the United Kingdom to give effect to the provisions of the Scheme and the suggestion of its supporters in regard thereto as early as possible by suitable legislation.

Government of India

(1) That a system of reserved and transferred subjects similar to that proposed for the provinces, shall be adopted for the Central Government.

(2) That the reserved subjects shall be foreign affairs (excepting relations with the colonies and dominions) army, navy, and relations with Indian Ruling Princes, and subject to the declaration of rights contained in resolution IV, the matters directly affecting public peace, tranquillity and defence of the country, and all other subjects shall be transferred subjects.

(V) (a) 'This Conference, while making due allowance for the necessities or drawbacks of transitional scheme, urges that, having regard to the terms of the announcement of August 20, 1917, and in order that the progress of India towards the goal of a self-governing unit of the British Empire may be facilitated and not unduly delayed or hampered, as also with a view to avoid the untoward consequences of a legislature containing a substantially elected popular element being allowed merely to indulge in criticism unchecked by responsibility, it

(3) The allotments required for reserved subjects should be the first charge on the revenues.

(4) The procedure for the adoption of the budget should be on the lines laid down for the provinces.

(5) All legislation should be by Bills introduced into the Legislative Assembly, provided that, if, in the case of reserved subjects, the Legislative Council does not pass such measures as the Government may deem necessary, the Governor General-in-Council may provide for the same by regulations, such regulations to be in force for one year but not to be renewed unless 40 per cent. of the members of the Assembly present and voting are in favour of them.

(6) There shall be no Council of State, but if the Council of State is to be constituted, at least half of its total strength shall consist of elected members, and that procedure by certification shall be confined to the reserved subjects.

(7) At least half the number of Executive Councillors (if there be more than one) in charge of reserved subjects should be Indians.

(8) The number of members of the Legislative Assembly should be raised to 150 and the proportion of the elected members should be four-fifths.

(9) The President and the Vice-President of the Legislative Assembly should be elected by the Assembly.

(10) The Legislative Assembly should have power to make or modify its own rules of business and they shall not require the sanction of the Governor General.

is essential that the principle of responsible government' should be introduced also in the Government of India, simultaneously with a similar reform in the provinces. There should, therefore, be a division of functions in the Central Government into 'reserved' and 'transferred' as a part of the present instalment of reforms and the Committee on division of functions should be instructed to investigate the subject and make recommendations.

(b) While, as suggested above, some measures of transfer of power to the Indian Legislature should be introduced at the commencement, provision should be made for future progress towards complete responsible government of the Government of India by specifically authorizing the proposed periodic Commissions to inquire into the matter and to recommend to Parliament such further advance as may be deemed necessary or desirable in that behalf.

(c) The power of certification given to the Governor-General should be limited to matters involving the defence of the country's foreign and political relations, and peace and order and should not be extended to 'good government' generally or 'sound financial administration.'

(e) This Conference recommends that the composition of the Council of State should be so altered as to ensure that one half of its total strength shall consist of elected members.

(f) The Indian element in the Executive Government of India should be one-half of the total number of that Government.

(11) There shall be an obligation to convene meetings of the Council and Assembly at stated intervals, or on the requistion of a certain proportion of members.

(12) A statutory guarantee should be given that full responsible government should be established in the whole of British India within a period not exceeding 15 years.

(13) That there should be no Privy Council for the present.

Provincial Governments

1. There should be no additional members of the Executive Government without portfolios.

2. From the commencement of the first Council the principle of responsibility of the ministers to the legislature shall come into force.

3. The status and salary of the ministers shall be the same as that of the members of Executive Council.

4. At least half the number of Executive Councillors in charge of reserved subjects (if there be more than one) should be Indians.

5. The Budget shall be under the control of the Legislature subject to the contribution to the Government of India, and during the life-time of the reformed Councils, to the allocation of a fixed sum for the reserved subjects; and should fresh taxation be necessary, it should be imposed by the provincial Governments, as a whole for both transferred and reserved subjects.

LEGISLATURE

1. While holding that the people are ripe for the introduc-

(e) The proposal to appoint an additional Member or Members from among the senior officials, without portfolios and without vote for purposes of consultation and advice only, but as *Members of the Executive Government*, in the provinces should be dropped.

(1)

(a) The status and emoluments of Ministers should be identical with those of Executive Councillors, and the Governor should not have greater power of control over them than over the latter.

(b) Whatever power may be given to the Governor-in-Council to interfere with the decisions of the Governor and Ministers on the ground of their possible effects on the administration of the reserved subjects, corresponding power should be given to the Governor and Ministers in respect of decisions of the Governor-in-Council affecting directly or indirectly the administration of the transferred subjects.

(d) Heads of provincial Governments in the major provinces should ordinarily be

tion of full provincial autonomy the Congress is yet prepared with a view to facilitating the passage of the Reforms, to leave the departments of Law, Police and Justice, (prisons excepted) in the hands of the Executive Government in all provinces for a period of six years. Executive and Judicial Departments must be separated at once.

2. The President and the Vice-President should be elected by the Council.

3. That the proposal to institute a Grand Committee shall be dropped. The Provincial Legislative Council shall legislate in respect of all matters within the jurisdiction of provincial Government, including Law, Justice and Police but where the Government is not satisfied with the decision of the Legislative Council in respect of matters relating to Law, Justice and Police, it shall be open to the Government to refer the matter to the Government of India. The Government of India may refer the matter to the Indian Legislature and the ordinary procedure shall follow. But if Grand Committees are instituted, this Congress is of opinion, that not less than one-half of the strength shall be elected by the Legislative Assembly.

4. The proportion of elected members in the Legislative Council shall be four fifths.

Elections

5. Whenever the Legislative Assembly, the Council of State, or the Legislative Council is dissolved, it shall be obligatory selected from the ranks of public men in the United Kingdom.

(e) No administrative control over subjects vested in provincial Governments should be 'reserved' in the central Government particularly in respect of 'transferred' heads.

(f) The Government of India should have no power to make a supplementary levy upon the provinces; they may only take loans from the latter on occasions of emergency.

(2) This Conference recommends that the largest possible number of subjects should be included in the 'transferred' list in every province as the progress and conditions of each province may justify and that none mentioned in the Illustrative List No. 11 appended to the Report should, as far as possible, be 'reserved' in any province.

IX (c) The Legislative Councils should have the right to elect their own Presidents and Vice-Presidents.

VIII (b) The elected element in the Provincial Legislative Councils should be four-fifths of the total strength of the Councils at least in the more advanced provinces.

IX. 1 (a) It should be provided that when a Council is dissolved by the Governor, a fresh election should be held and the new Council summoned not later than four months after the dissolution.

VIII (a) The Franchise should be as wide and the composition of the Legislative Council should be as liberal as circumstances may admit in each province, the number of representatives of the general territorial electorates

on the Government as the case may be, to order the necessary elections, and to resummon the body dissolved within a period of three months from the date of dissolution.

6. The Legislative Assembly should have power to make or modify its own rules of business and they shall not require the sanction of the Governor-General.

7. There should be an obligation to convene meetings of the Council and Assembly at stated intervals, or on the requisition of a certain proportion of members of the Assembly.

8. No dissolution of the legislature shall take place except by way of an appeal to the electorate and the reason shall be stated in writing countersigned by the Ministers.

being fixed in every case at not less than one-half of the whole council.

(c) The franchise should be so broad and the electorates so devised as to secure to all classes of tax-payers their due representation by election and the interests of those communities or groups of communities in Madras and the Bombay Deccan and elsewhere who at present demand special electoral protection should be adequately safeguarded by introducing a system of plural constituencies in which a reasonable number of seats should be reserved for those communities.

(e) In the case of any community for which separate special electorates may be deemed at present necessary, participation in the general territorial electorates, whether as voters or candidates, should not be permitted.

(f) It shall be left to the option of an individual belonging to a community which is given separate representation to enrol himself as a voter either in the general or the communal electorate.

Parliament and India Office

(e) The control of Parliament and of the Secretary of State must only be modified as the responsibility of the Indian and provincial Governments to the electorates is increased. No power over provincial Governments now exercised by Parliament and by the Secretary of State must be transferred to the Government of India, save in matters of routine administra-

(XI) This Conference, while generally approving of the proposals embodied in the Report regarding the India Office and Parliamentary control, urges:—

(a) That the administrative control of Parliament over the Government of India exercised through the Secretary of State should continue except in so far as the control of the legislature on the spot is substituted for

tion until the latter is responsible to the electorates.

(d) No financial or administrative powers in regard to reserved subjects should be transferred to the provincial Governments until such time as they are made responsible regarding them to electorates, and until then the control of Parliament and the Secretary of State should continue.

(b) The Council of India shall be abolished, and there shall be two permanent Under-secretaries to assist the Secretary of State for India, one of whom shall be an Indian.

(c) All charges in respect to the India Office establishment shall be placed on the British estimates.

(d) The committee to be appointed to examine and report on the present constitution of the Council of India shall contain an adequate Indian element.

the present Parliamentary control.

(d) That until the India Council can be abolished by substituting Indian control for the control of Parliament over the affairs of India, it should be a mere advisory body with its strength reduced to 8 members, four of whom should be Indians.

(c) That at least a major part of the cost of the India Office should be borne by the British Exchequer.

(b) That Indian opinion should be represented on the Committee appointed to report upon the organisation of the India Office and the evidence of Indian witnesses invited.

Mahomedan Representation

Resolution VII. The proportion of Mahomedans in the Legislative Council and the Legislative Assembly as laid down in the Congress-League Scheme must be maintained.

(VIII) (d) Mahomedan representation in every legislature should be in the proportions mentioned in the Scheme adopted by the Congress and the Muslim League at Lucknow in 1916.

Army Commissions

Resolution XII. This Congress places on record its deep disappointment at the altogether inadequate response made by the Government to the demand for the grant of commissions to Indians in the army, and is of opinion that steps should be immediately taken so as to enable the grant to Indians at

(b) This Conference strongly urges that Indians should be nominated to 20 per cent., to start with, of King's commissions in the Indian Army and that adequate provision for training them should be made in this country itself.

an early date of at least 25 per cent. of the commissions in the army, the proportions to be gradually increased to 50 per cent. within a period of ten years.

Public Services

Resolution XVII. That this Congress is of opinion that the proportion of annual recruitment to the Indian civil service to be made in England should be 50 per cent. to start with, such recruitment to be by open competition in India from persons already appointed to the Provincial Civil Service.

X (a) This Conference thanks the Secretary of State and the Viceroy for recommending that all racial bars should be abolished and for recognizing the principle of recruiting of all the Indian public services in India and in England instead of any service being recruited for exclusively in the latter country.

Franchise for Women

Resolution VIII. Women possessing the same qualifications as are laid down for men in any part of the Scheme shall not be disqualified on account of sex.

Constitution of Councils

Resolution XIII. That, so far as the question of determining the franchise and the constituence and the composition of the Legislative Assemblies is concerned, this Congress is of opinion that, instead of being left to be dealt with by Committees, it should be decided by the House of Commons and be incorporated in the statute to be framed for the constitution of the Indian Government.

Resolution XIV. That as regards the Committee to advise on the question of the separation of Indian from provincial functions and also with regard to the Committee if any for the con-

Constitution of Periodic Commission

9 (b) Some provision should be made for the appointment and cooperation of qualified Indians on the periodic commission proposed to be appointed every ten or twelve years and it should further be provided that the first periodic commission shall come to India and submit its recommendations to Parliament before the expiry of the third Legislative Council after the Reform Scheme comes into operation and that every subsequent periodic commission should be appointed at the end of every ten years.

sideration of reserved or an unreserved department, this Congress is of opinion that the principle set forth in the above resolution should apply *mutatis mutandis* to the formation of the said Committee.

Or

In the alternative; if a Committee is appointed for the purpose, the two non-official members of the Committee should be elected — one by the All-India Congress Committee and the other by the Council of the Moslem League while the coopted non-official for each province should be elected by the Provincial Congress Committee of that province.

The All-India Muslim League is in substantial accord with the resolutions of the Special Congress. It will be easily seen that Indian opinion, of both Hindus and Mussulmans, is substantially in accord in their demands for the democratization of the Central government and in their criticism of the rest of the scheme. The Indians have thus exercised their right of self-determination through their popular bodies and are entitled to get what they demand. After all, what they ask for is only a modest instalment of autonomy under British control.

In the appendices the reader will find a comparative table showing (a) the present Constitution of Government in India (b) the proposals of the Secretary of State and the Viceroy (c) and the Congress League Scheme.

XI

INDIA'S CLAIM TO FISCAL AUTONOMY "INDUSTRIES AND TARIFFS"

> . . . . for equality of right amongst nations, small as well as great, is one of the fundamental issues this country and her allies are fighting to establish in this war.
>
> DAVID LLOYD GEORGE
>
> "The War Aims of the Allies." Speech delivered to delegates of the Trade Unions, at the Central Hall, Westminster, January 5, 1918.

> I beg to record my strong opinion that in the matter of Indian industries we are bound to consider Indian interests firstly, secondly, and thirdly. I mean by "firstly" that the local raw products should be utilised, by secondly, that industries should be introduced and by "thirdly" that the profits of such industry should remain in the country.
>
> SIR FREDERICK NICHOLSON
>
> Quoted on page 300, Report of the Indian Industrial Commission, 1916–1918.

ECONOMIC bondage is the worst of all bondages. Economic dependence, or the lack of economic independence, is the source of all misery, individual or national. A person economically dependent upon another is a virtual slave, despite appearances. He who supplies food and raiment and the necessities of life is the real master.

The desire for gain dominates the world and all its activities. Even religion, as ordinarily understood, interpreted and administered, is a game of pounds and shillings, say what one may to the contrary. There are exceptions to this statement, but they are few and far between. The world does not subsist by bread alone, but without bread it cannot exist even for a minute. The generality of the world cares more for bread than for anything else, though there are individuals and groups of individuals who would not stoop to obtain bread by dishonorable means and those also who would die rather than obtain bread by the violation of their soul.

There are numerous ways in which a subject nation feels the humiliation and helplessness of her position, but none is so telling and so effective as the subordination of her economic interests to those of the dominant power. This is especially true in these days of free and easy transportation, of quick journeys, and of scientific warfare. In any struggle between nations, the victory eventually must rest with the one in possession of the largest number of "silver bullets." It is true that silver bullets alone will not do unless there are brains and bodies to use them, but the latter without the former are helpless.

A nation may be the greatest producer of food; yet she may die of hunger from lack of ability to keep her own produce for herself. Food obeys the behest of the silver bullets. The law of self-preservation, therefore, requires only that nations be free to regulate their own household, subject to the condition that thereby they do not violate the rules of humanity or trample upon the rights of any human being.

Mr. Montagu and Lord Chelmsford have, in parts of their Report, been extremely candid. The value of their joint production lies in this candidness. In no other part, perhaps, have they been so candid as in the one dealing with "Industries and Tariff." In Paragraph 331 they frankly admit the truth of the following observation of the late Mr. Ranade on the economic effects of British rule in India:

> "The political domination of one country by another attracts far more attention than the more formidable, though more unfelt, domination which the capital, enterprise and skill of one country exercise over the trade and manufactures of another. This latter domination has an insidious influence which paralyses the springs of all the various activities which together make up the life of a nation."

In the course of a letter addressed to the *Westminster Gazette* in 1917, Lord Curzon said that "the fiscal policy of India during the last thirty or forty years has been shaped far more in Manchester than in Calcutta." This candid admission about "the subordination of Indian fiscal policy to the Secretary of State and a House of Commons powerfully affected by Lancashire influence," is the keynote of the Indian demand for Home Rule. The authors of the Montagu-Chelmsford Report say so quite frankly and fairly in Paragraphs 332 to 336 of their report, from which we make the following extracts:

"The people are poor; and their poverty raises the question whether the general level of well-being could not be materially raised by the development of industries. It is also clear that the lack of outlet for educated youth is a serious misfortune which has contributed not a little in the past to political unrest in Bengal. But perhaps an even greater mischief is the discontent aroused in the minds of those who are jealous for India by seeing that she is so largely dependent on foreign countries for manufactured goods. They noted that her foreign trade was always growing, but they also saw that its leading feature continued to be the barter of raw materials valued at relatively low prices for imported manufactures, which obviously afforded profits and prosperity to other countries industrially more advanced. Patriotic Indians might well ask themselves why these profits should not accrue to their country: and also why so large a portion of the industries which flourished in the country was financed by European capital and managed by European skill."

"The fact that India's foreign trade was largely with the United Kingdom gave rise to a suspicion that her industrial backwardness was positively encouraged in the interests of British manufactures, and the maintenance of the excise duty on locally manufactured cotton goods in the alleged interests of Lancashire is very widely accepted as a conclusive proof of such a purpose. On a smaller scale, the maintenance of a Stores Department at the India Office is looked upon as an encouragement to the Government to patronize British at the expense of local manufacturers."

There can thus be no autonomy without fiscal autonomy. In fact, the latter alone is the determining characteristic of an autonomous existence.

The one national trait which distinguishes the British from other nations of the world is their habit of truthfulness and frankness. When we say that we do not thereby mean that all Britishers are equally truthful — to the same extent and degree. But we do mean that on the whole the British nation has a larger percentage of truthful and candid persons in her family than any other nation on the face of the earth. Where their interests clash with those of others, they can be as hard, exacting and cruel as any one else in the world. But repentance overtakes them sooner than it does the others. They have a queer but admirable faculty of introspection which few other people possess to the same extent and in the same numbers. This is what endears them even to those who are never tired of cursing their snobbishness and masterful imperialism. The faculty of occasionally seeing themselves with the eyes of others, makes them the most successful *rulers of men.* They are as a nation lacking in imagination, but there are individuals amongst them who can see, if they will, their own faults; who can and do speak out their minds honestly and truthfully, even though by so doing they may temporarily earn odium and unpopularity.

The remarks and observations of the eminent authors of the Report relating to the fiscal relations of India and England reflect the honesty of their purpose and the sincerity of their mind as no other part of the Report does. They have entered upon the subject with great diffidence and, though expressing themselves with marked candor and fairness, have refrained from making any definite recommendations.

In this respect it will be only fair to acknowledge the equally candid opinion of Mr. Austin Chamberlain, who, in 1917, made a most significant confession by stating on an important occasion that "India will not remain, and ought not to remain content to be a hewer of wood and a drawer of water for the rest of the Empire."

To our simple minds, not accustomed to the anomalies of official life, it seems inexplicable how, after these candid admissions, the authors could have any hesitation in recommending the only remedy by which India's wrong could be righted and her economic rights secured in the future — viz., fiscal autonomy.

In Paragraph 335 the authors of the report give the genesis of the Swadeshi boycott movement of 1905, and very pertinently observe that "in Japanese progress and efficiency" the educated Indians see "an example of what could be effected by an Asiatic nation free of foreign control," or in other words, of what could be achieved by India, if she had a national government of her own interested in her industrial advance. Mr. Montagu and Lord Chelmsford thus rightly observe that "English theories to the appropriate limits of the State's activity are inapplicable in India" and that if the resources of the country are to be developed the Government must take action.

"After the war," add the authors, "the need for industrial development will be all the greater unless India is to become a mere dumping-ground for the manufactures of foreign nations which will then be competing all the more keenly for the markets on which their political strength so perceptibly depends. India will certainly consider herself entitled to claim all the help that her Government can give her to enable her to take her place as a manufacturing country; and unless the claim is admitted it will surely turn into an insistent request for a tariff which will penalize imported articles without respect of origin."

Further on the Report states:

"We are agreed therefore that there must be a definite change of view; and that the Government must admit and shoulder its responsibility for furthering the industrial development of the country. The difficulties by this time are well-known. In the past, and partly as a result of recent *swadeshi* experiences, India's capital has not generally been readily available; among some communities at least there is apparent distaste for practical training, and a comparative weakness of mutual trust; *skilled labour is lacking*, and although *labour is plentiful, education is needed to inculcate a higher standard of living and so to secure a continuous supply; there is a dearth of technical institutions; there is also a want of practical information about the commercial potentialities of India's war products.* Though these are serious difficulties, they are not insuperable; but they will be overcome only if the State comes forward boldly as guide and helper. On the other hand, there are good grounds for hope. India has great natural resources, mineral and vegetable. She has furnished supplies of manganese, tungsten, mica, jute, copra, lac, etc., for use in the war. She has abundant coal, even if its geographical distribution is uneven; she has also in her large rivers ample means of creating water-power. There is good reason for believing that she will greatly increase her output of oil. Her forest wealth is immense, and much of it only awaits the introduction of modern means of transportation, a bolder investment of capital, and the employment of extra staff; while the patient and laborious work of conservation that has been steadily proceeding joined with modern scientific methods of improving supplies and increasing output, will yield a rich harvest in the future. We have been assured that Indian capital will be forthcoming once it is realized that it can be invested with security and profit in India; a purpose that will be furthered by the provision of increased facilities for banking and credit. Labor, though abundant, is handicapped by still pursuing uneconomical methods, and its output would be greatly increased by the extended use of machinery. We have no doubt that there is an immense scope for the application of scientific methods. Conditions are ripe for the development of new and for the revival of old industries, and the real enthusiasm for industries which is not confined to the ambitions of a few individuals but rests on the general desire to see Indian capital and labour applied jointly to the good of the country, seem to us the happiest augury."

The views of educated India about fiscal policy have been very faithfully reproduced in Paragraphs 341 and 342, which also we reproduce almost bodily:

"Connected intimately with the matter of industries is the question of the Indian tariff. This subject was excluded from the deliberations of the Industrial Commission now sitting because it was not desirable at that juncture to raise any question of the modification of India's fiscal policy; but its exclusion was none the less the object of some legitimate criticism in India. The changes which we propose in the Government of India will still leave the settlement of India's tariff in the hands of a government amenable to Parliament and the Secretary of State; but inasmuch as the tariff reacts on many matters which will henceforth come more and more under Indian control, we think it well that we should put forward for the information of His Majesty's Government the views of educated Indians upon this subject. We have no immediate proposals to make; we are anxious merely that any decisions which may hereafter be taken should be taken with full appreciation of educated Indian opinion.

"The theoretical free trader, we believe, hardly

exists in India at present. As was shown by the debates in the Indian Legislative Council in March, 1913, educated Indian opinion ardently desires a tariff. It rightly wishes to find another substantial basis than that of the land for Indian revenues, and it turns to a tariff to provide one. Desiring industries which will give him Indian-made clothes to wear and Indian-made articles to use, the educated Indian looks to the example of other countries which have relied on tariffs, and seizes on the admission of even free traders that for the nourishment of nascent industries a tariff is permissible. We do not know whether he pauses to reflect that these industries will be largely financed by foreign capital attracted by the tariff, although we have evidence that he has not learned to appreciate the advantages of foreign capital. But whatever economic fallacy underlies his reasoning, these are his firm beliefs; and though he may be willing to concede the possibility that he is wrong, he will not readily concede that it is our business to decide the matter for him. He believes that as long as we continue to decide for him we shall decide in the interests of England and not according to his wishes; and he points to the debate in the House of Commons on the differentiation of the cotton excise in support of his contention. So long as the people who refuse India protection are interested in manufactures with which India might compete, Indian opinion cannot bring itself to believe that the refusal is disinterested or dictated by care for the best interests of India. This real and keen desire for fiscal autonomy does not mean that educated opinion in India is unmindful of Imperial obligations. . . ."

These admissions should put India's claims for fiscal autonomy beyond the range of doubt and dispute, but so strange are the ways of modern statesmanship that consistency and logic are not the necessary accompaniments thereof.

The authors have advanced another very strong argument for the economic development of India, viz., "military value," which makes the case conclusive. This argument has been supplied by the Great War and is so well known that we need not state it in their words.

If India is to prosper and take her legitimate place in the British Commonwealth, and in the great family of Nations of the World, it is absolutely necessary that she should be given complete fiscal freedom to manage her own affairs, develop her own industries and do her own trading. Considering her size and resources, it wounds her self-respect and makes her feel exceedingly mean and small to go begging for alms and charity every time there is a failure of rains and the cry of famine is raised.

For a nation of 315 millions of human beings living in a country which nature has endowed with all its choicest blessings, rich and fertile soil, plenty of water and sun, an abundant supply of metals and coal, willing labor, artistic skill and a power of manipulating for beauty and elegance unexcelled in the world — to exist in pitiful economic dependence is a condition most deplorable and most pathetic. We want no charity, no concessions, no favors, no preference. What we most earnestly beg and ask for is an *opportunity*.

For a synopsis of the findings and recommendations of the Industrial Commission mentioned in this chapter see appendix 1.

XII

THE REVOLUTIONARY MOVEMENT

In December, 1917, the Government of India appointed a committee of three Englishmen and two Indians (1) "to investigate and report on the nature and extent of the criminal conspiracies connected with the revolutionary movements in India, (2) to examine and consider the difficulties that have arisen in dealing with such conspiracies and to advise as to the legislation, if any, necessary to enable the government to deal effectively with them." Of the three English members, Mr. Justice Rowlatt of the King's Bench Division, England, was appointed as president, and of the other two, one was a judge in the service of the Government and the other a member of a Board of Revenue in one of the Indian Provinces. Of the two Indians, one was a judge and the other a practicing lawyer.

This committee submitted its report in April, 1918, which was published by the Government of India in July of the same year. The president, Mr. Justice Rowlatt's letter covering the report gives the nature of the evidence upon which their report is based, which is as follows: "Statements have been placed before us with documentary evidence by the Governments of Bengal, Bombay, Bihar and Orissa, the Central Provinces, the United Provinces, the Punjab and Burmah as well as by the Government of India. In every case, except that of Madras, we were further attended by officers of the government, presenting this statement, who gave evidence before us. In the two provinces in which we held sittings, namely, Bengal and Punjab, we further invited and secured the attendance of individuals, or as deputed by associations, of gentlemen who we thought might give us information from various non-official points of view."

It is clear from this statement that the investigation of the committee was neither judicial nor even semi-judicial; it was a purely administrative inquiry conducted behind the backs of the individuals concerned, without the latter having any opportunity of cross-examining the witnesses or giving their explanations of the evidence against them. While the different Governments in India were fully represented in each case by the ablest of their servants, the individuals investigated were not. We do not want to insinuate that either the Governments or the officers deputed by them were unfair in their evidence. All that we want to point out is that the other side had no opportunity of putting their case before the committee. Consequently, it is no wonder that one comes across many traces of political and racial bias both in the introduction and the Report.

The very first paragraph of the introduction betrays either ignorance on the part of the committee about the ancient history of India, or a deliberate misrepresentation of the nature of the Hindu State. The committee says: "Republican or Parliamentary forms of governments as at present understood were neither desired nor known in India until after the establishment of British rule. In the Hindu State the form of government was an absolute monarchy, though the monarch was by the Hindu Shastras hedged round by elaborate rules for securing the welfare of his subjects and was assisted by a body of councillors, the chief of whom were Brahmin members of the priestly class which derived authority from a time when the priests were the sole repositories of knowledge and therefore the natural instruments of administration." The statements made in this paragraph do not represent the whole truth.

The committee ignores the fact that Republican or Parliamentary forms of Government "*as at present understood*" were neither desired nor known in any part of the world, except perhaps England itself until *after* the establishment of British rule in India.[1] Then the committee has altogether ignored that, in the Hindu State, the form of government was not an absolute monarchy *always and in all parts of India.* There is ample historical evidence to prove that India had many Republican States, along with oligarchies and monarchies at one and the same period of her history. The second part of the second sentence is also not correct, because the priestly class derived its authority from a time when the priests were not the sole repositories of knowledge. The several Hindu political treatises belong to a period when the whole populace was highly educated and could take substantial part in the determination of the affairs of their country.

Equally misleading is the last sentence of the introduction where the committee says that it is among the

[1] The beginnings of British rule in India were made in 1757 A.D.

Chitpavan Brahmins of the Poona district that they first find indications of a revolutionary movement. This statement is incorrect, if it means that after the establishment of British rule in India no attempt had been made to overthrow it prior to the Revolutionary movement inaugurated by the Poona Brahmins. The statement ignores three such attempts which are known to history; viz., (*a*) the great Mutiny of 1857, (*b*) the Wahábee Rebellion of Bengal, and (*c*) the Kúká Rebellion of the Punjab; not to mention other minor attempts made in other places by other people.

Yet we think that this report is a very valuable document, giving in one place the history and the progress of the Revolutionary Movement in India. The findings and the recommendations of the committee may not be all correct, but the material collected and published for the first time is too valuable to be neglected by anyone who wants to have an intelligent grasp of the political situation in India, such as has developed within the last twenty years.

The committee gives a summary of its conclusions as to the conspiracies in Chapter XV, which we copy verbatim:

"In Bombay they have been purely Brahmin and mostly Chitpavan. In Bengal the conspirators have been young men belonging to the educated middle classes. Their propaganda has been elaborate, persistent and ingenious. In their own province it has produced a long series of murders and robberies. In Bihar and Orissa, the United Provinces, the Central Provinces and Madras, it took no root, but occasionally led to crime and disorder. In the Punjab the return of emigrants from America, bent on revolution and bloodshed, produced numerous outrages and the

Ghadr conspiracy of 1915. In Burma, too, the *Ghadr* movement was active, but was arrested.

"Finally came a Mohammedan conspiracy confined to a small clique of fanatics and designed to overthrow British rule with foreign aid.

"All these plots have been directed towards one and the same objective, the overthrow by force of British rule in India. Sometimes they have been isolated; sometimes they have been interconnected; sometimes they have been encouraged and supported by German influence. All have been successfully encountered with the support of Indian loyalty."

In this general summary the committee has made no attempt to trace out the causes that led to the inauguration of the revolutionary movement and its subsequent progress. A chapter on that subject would have been most illuminating.

In chapters dealing with provinces they have selected some individuals and classes on whom to lay blame for "incitements" to murders and crimes, but have entirely failed to analyze the social, political and economic conditions which made such incitements and their success possible.

It is clear even from this summary that the only two provinces where the revolutionary propaganda took root and resulted in more than occasional outrages were Bengal and the Punjab.

In the Bombay Presidency, revolutionary outrages did not exceed three within a period of 20 years (from 1897 to 1917), two murders and one bomb-throwing. Besides, three trials for conspiracies are mentioned all within a year (1909–1910), two in Native States and one in British territory. Altogether 82 men were prosecuted for being involved in these conspiracies.

The total result comes to this, that in the course of 20 years about 100 persons were found to be involved in a revolutionary movement in a territory embracing an area of 186,923 square miles and a population of 27 million human beings. This is surely by no means a formidable record justifying extraordinary legislation such as is proposed.[1] The net loss of human life did not exceed three, though unfortunately all three victims were Europeans.

Bihar and Orissa formed part of the province of Bengal during most of the period covered by the revolutionary movement of Bengal, viz., from 1906 to 1917. It was in Bihar which was then a part of Bengal, that in 1908, the first bomb was thrown. The only other revolutionary outrage that took place in Bihar was one in 1913, resulting in the murder of two Indians.

In the United Provinces of Agra and Oude, the only tangible evidence of revolutionary activity recorded by the committee is the Benares Conspiracy that came to light in 1915–1916. The only outrage noted is that of the alleged murder of a fellow revolutionary by a member of the same gang.

To the Central provinces the committee has given a practically clean bill.

In Madras the revolutionary outrages consisted of one murder (of a European Magistrate) and one conspiracy involving nine persons.

The cons acies and intrigues detected in Burma are ascribed to people of other provinces and not a single outrage from that province itself is reported.

So we find that in the period from 1906 to 1907,

[1] Since enacted.

both inclusive, outside the provinces of Bengal and the Punjab, the revolutionary crime was limited to three outrages and three conspiracies in the Bombay Presidency, one outrage in Bihar, one outrage and one conspiracy in the United Provinces, one outrage and one conspiracy in Madras and some intrigues and conspiracies during the war in Burma. Thus the only two provinces in which the revolutionary movement established itself to any appreciable extent was Bengal and the Punjab.

In the Punjab, again, the first revolutionary crime took place in December, 1912, and the second in 1913 and the rest all during the War. Cases of seditious utterances and writings are not included in the term "revolutionary crime" used in the above paragraphs. It was from Bengal, then, that before the War revolutionary propaganda was carried on to any large extent, revolutionary movements organized and revolutionary crimes committed. About half of the Report deals with Bengal and the general findings of the committee may be thus summarized:

(1) That the object of the movement was the overturning of "the British government in India by violent means" (p. 15 and also p. 19).

(2) That the class among whom the movement spread was comprised of the *Bhadralok* (the respectable middle class). The committee says:

"The people among whom he (i.e., Barendra, the first Bengali revolutionary propagandist) worked, the *bhadralok* of Bengal, have been for centuries peaceful and unwarlike, but, through the influence of the great central city of Calcutta, were early in appreciating the advantages of Western learning. They are mainly

Hindus and their leading castes are Brahmins, Kayasthas and Vaidyas; but with the spread of English education some other castes too have adopted *bhadralok* ideals and modes of life. *Bhadralok* abound in villages as well as in towns, and are thus more interwoven with the landed classes than are the literate Indians of other provinces. Wherever they live or settle, they earnestly desire and often provide English education for their sons. The consequence is that a number of Anglo-vernacular schools, largely maintained by private enterprise, have sprung up throughout the towns and villages of Bengal. No other province of India possesses a network of rural schools in which English is taught. These schools are due to the enterprise of the *bhadralok* and to the fact that, as British rule gradually spread from Bengal over Northern India, the scope of employment for English-educated Bengalis spread with it. Originally they predominated in all offices and higher grade schools throughout Upper India. They were also, with the Parsees, the first Indians to send their sons to England for education, to qualify for the Bar, or to compete for the higher grades of the Civil and Medical services. When, however, similar classes in other provinces also acquired a working knowledge of English, the field for Bengali enterprise gradually shrank. In their own province *bhadralok* still almost monopolize the clerical and subordinate administrative services of Government. They are prominent in medicine, in teaching and at the Bar. But, in spite of these advantages, they have felt the shrinkage of foreign employment; and as the education which they receive is generally literary and ill-adapted to incline the youthful mind to industrial, commercial or agricultural pursuits, they have not succeeded in finding fresh outlets for their energies. Their hold on land, too, has weakened, owing to increasing pressure of population and excessive sub-infeudation. *Altogether their economic prospects have narrowed, and the increasing numbers who draw fixed incomes have felt the pinch of rising prices. On the other hand, the memories and associations of their earlier prosperity, combined with growing contact with Western ideas and standards of comfort, have raised their expectations of the pecuniary remuneration which should reward a laborious and, to their minds, a costly education.* Thus as *bhadralok* learned in English have become more and more numerous, a growing number have become less and less inclined to accept the conditions of life in which they found themselves on reaching manhood. *Bhadralok* have always been prominent among the supporters of Indian political movements; and their leaders have watched with careful attention events in the world outside India. The large majority of the people of Bengal are not *bhadralok* but cultivators, and in the eastern districts mainly Muhammadans; but the cultivators of the province are absorbed in their own pursuits, in litigation, and in religious and caste observances. It was not to them but to his own class that Barendra appealed. When he renewed his efforts in 1904, the thoughts of many members of this class had been stirred by various powerful influences." [The italics are ours.]

We have given this lengthy extract as it shows conclusively (*a*) that the movement originated and spread among people who had received Western education, most of the leaders having been educated in England and (*b*) that the root cause of the movement was *economic.*

(3) That various circumstances occasioned by certain Government measures "specially favored the development" of the movement (p. 16). Among the measures specially mentioned are (*a*) the University law of Lord Curzon "which was interpreted by politicians as designed to limit the numbers of Indians educated in English and thus to retard national advance"; (*b*) the partition of Bengal by Lord Curzon. "It was the

agitation that attended and followed on this measure that brought previous discontent to a climax."

(4) That the revolutionary movement received a substantial impetus by the failure of constitutional agitation for the reversal of the policy that decided on partitioning Bengal into two divisions. This failure led to two different kinds of agitation, open and secret: (*a*) open economic defiance by *Swadeshi* and boycott—*Swadeshi* was the affirmative and boycott the negative form of the same movement. *Swadeshi* enjoined the use of country made articles; boycott was directed against English imports, (*b*) open propaganda by a more outspoken and in some instances violent press, (*c*) open control of educational agencies by means of national institutions, (*d*) open stimulus to physical education and physical culture, (*e*) nationalistic interpretation of religious dogma and forms (open), (*f*) organization of secret societies for more violent propaganda, for learning and teaching the use of firearms, for the manufacture of bombs, for illicit purchase and stealing of firearms, for assassination and murder, (*g*) secret attempts to tamper with the army, (*h*) conspiracies for terroristic purposes and for obtaining sinews of war by theft, robbery and extortion.

The following two extracts which the committee has taken from one of the publications of the revolutionary party called *Mukti Kon Pathe* (what is the path of salvation) will explain clauses (*f*) and (*g*) and (*h*).

"The book further points out that not much muscle was required to shoot Europeans, that arms could be procured by grim determination, and that weapons could be prepared silently in some secret place. Indians could be sent to foreign countries to learn the art of making weapons. The assistance of Indian soldiers must be obtained. They must be made to understand the misery and wretchedness of the country. The heroism of Sivaji must be remembered. As long as revolutionary work remained in its infancy, expenses could be met by subscriptions. But as work advanced, money must be extracted from society by the application of forcc. If the revolution is being brought about for the welfare of society, then it is perfectly just to collect money from society for that purpose. It is admitted that theft and dacoity are crimes because they violate the principle of good society. But the political dacoit is aiming at the good of society, "so no sin but rather virtue attaches to the destruction of this small good for the sake of some higher good. Therefore if revolutionaries extort money from the miserly or luxurious members of society by the application of force, their conduct is perfectly just."

Mukti Kon Pathe further exhorts its readers to obtain the "help of the native soldiers. . . . Although these soldiers for the sake of their stomach accept service in the Government of the ruling power, still they are nothing but men made of flesh and blood. They, too, know (how) to think; when therefore the revolutionaries explain to them the woes and miseries of the country, they, in proper time, swell the ranks of the revolutionaries with arms and weapons given them by the ruling power. . . . Because it is possible to persuade the soldiers in this way, the modern English Raj of India does not allow the cunning Bengalis to enter into the ranks of the army. . . . Aid in the shape of arms may be secretly obtained by securing the help of the foreign ruling powers."

(5) That except in five cases the idea of private gain never entered into the activities of the revolu-

tionaries and of the five persons referred to three were taxi-cab drivers either hired or coerced to coöperate in revolutionary enterprise (p. 20).

(6) That "the circumstances that robberies and murders are being committed by young men of respectable extraction, students at schools and colleges, is indeed an amazing phenomenon the occurrence of which in most countries would be hardly credible."

(7) That "since the year 1906 revolutionary outrages in Bengal have numbered 210 and attempts at committing such outrages have amounted to 101. Definite information is in the hands of the police of the complicity of no less than 1038 persons in these offences. But of these, only 84 persons have been convicted of specified crimes in 39 prosecutions, and of these persons, 30 were tried by tribunals constituted under the Defence of India Act. Ten attempts have been made to strike at revolutionary conspiracies by means of prosecutions directed against groups or branches. In these prosecutions 192 persons were involved, 63 of whom were convicted. Eighty-two revolutionaries have rendered themselves liable to be bound over to be of good behaviour under the preventive sections of the Criminal Procedure Code. In regard to 51 of these, there is direct evidence of complicity in outrages. There have, moreover, been 59 prosecutions under the Arms and Explosives Acts which have resulted in convictions of 58 persons."

We wish the committee had also supplemented this information by a complete record of the punishments that were imposed on persons convicted of revolutionary crime in the ten years from 1906 to 1917. We are sure such a statement would have been most informing and illuminating. It would have conclusively established the soundness of the half-hearted finding that "the convictions . . . did not have as much effect as might have been expected in repressing crime." In fact they had no effect. They only added fuel to the fire.

(8) That persons involved in revolutionary crime belonged to all castes and occupations and the vast bulk of them were non-Brahmins. They were of all ages, from 10–15 to over 45, the majority being under 25. The committee has in an appendix (p. 93) given three tables of statistics as to age, caste, occupation or profession of persons convicted in Bengal of revolutionary crimes or killed in commission of such crimes during the years 1907–1917. This clause is based on these statistics.

We are afraid, however, that these statistics do not afford quite a correct index of the age, caste, occupation and position of all the people in Bengal that were and are sympathetically interested in the revolutionary movement of Bengal.

In investigating reasons for failure of ordinary machinery for the prevention, detection and punishment of crime in Bengal, the committee has assigned six reasons: (*a*) want of evidence, (*b*) paucity of police, (*c*) facilities enjoyed by criminals, (*d*) difficulty in proof of possession of arms, etc., (*e*) distrust of evidence, (*f*) the uselessness, in general, of confession made to the Police. These reasons, however, do not represent the whole truth. Some of the most daring crimes were committed in broad daylight, in much frequented streets of the metropolis and in the presence of numerous people. Moreover, the Government did not depend on ordinary law. Measure after measure was enacted to expedite and facilitate convictions. Extraordinary provisions were made to meet all the difficulties pointed out by the committee and extraordinary sentences were given in the case of conviction. Yet the Government failed either to extirpate the movement or to check it effectively or to bring the majority of offenders to book.

The members of the committee have frankly admitted: "That we do not expect very much from punitive measures. The conviction of offenders will never check such a movement as that which grew up in Bengal unless the leaders can be convicted at the outset." They pin their faith on "preventive" measures recommended by them. It was perhaps not within their scope to say that the most effective preventive measure was the removal of the political and economic causes that had generated the movement. The committee has studiously avoided discussing that important point, but now and then they have incidentally furnished the real clue to the situation. Discussing the "accessibility of Bengal schools and colleges to Revolutionary influences," they quote a passage from one of the reports of the Director of Public Instruction in Bengal. We copy below the whole of this paragraph, as, to us, it seems to be very pertinent to the issue.

"*Accessibility of Bengal Schools and Colleges to Revolutionary Influences.* — Abundant evidence has compelled us to the conclusion that the secondary English schools, and in a less degree the colleges, of Bengal have been regarded by the revolutionaries as their most fruitful recruiting centres. Dispersed as these schools are far and wide throughout the Province, sometimes clustering in a town, sometimes isolated in the far-away villages of the eastern water-country, they form natural objects for attack; and as is apparent from the reports of the Department of Public Instruction, they have been attacked for years with no small degree of success. In these reports the Director has from time to time noticed such matters as the circulation of seditious leaflets, the number of students implicated in conspiracy cases and the apathy of parents and guardians. But perhaps his most instructive passages are the following, in which he sets out the whole situation in regard to secondary English schools. 'The number of these schools,' he wrote, 'is rapidly increasing, and the cry is for more and more. It is a demand for tickets in a lottery, the prizes of which are posts in Government service and employment in certain professions. *The bhadralok have nothing to look to but these posts*, while those who desire to rise from a lower social or economic station have their eyes on the same goal. *The middle classes in Bengal are generally poor, and the increased stress of competition and the tendency for the average earnings of certain careers to decrease* — a tendency which is bound to follow on the increased demand to enter them, *coupled with the rise in the cost of living and the inevitable raising in the standard of comfort — all these features continue to make the struggle to exist in these classes keener.* Hence the need to raise educational standards, to make school life a greater influence for good and the course of instruction more thorough and more comprehensive. A need which becomes more and more imperative as life in India becomes more complicated and more exacting is confronted by a determined though perfectly natural opposition to the raising of fees. . . . *Probably the worst feature of the situation is the low wages and the complete absence of prospects which are the fate of teachers in the secondary schools.* . . . It is easy to blame the parents for blindness to their sons' true good, but the matriculation examination is the thing that seems to matter, so that if his boy passes the annual promotion examinations and is duly presented at that examination at the earliest possible date, the average parent has no criticism to offer. This is perfectly natural, but the future of Bengal depends to a not inconsiderable extent on the work done in its secondary schools, and more is required of these institutions than an ability to pass a certain proportion of boys through the Calcutta University Matriculation examination. . . . The present condition of secondary schools is undoubtedly prejudicing the development of the presidency and is by no means a negligible feature in the existing state of general disturbance. It is customary to trace the genesis of much sedition and crime to the back streets and lanes of Calcutta and Dacca, where the organizers of anarchic conspiracies seek their agents from among University students. This view is correct as far as it goes, but it is in the high schools, with their underpaid and discontented teachers, their crowded, dark and ill-ventilated classrooms, and their soul-destroying process of unceasing cram, that the seeds of discontent and fanaticism are sown." [The italics are ours.]

Yet for years nothing was done to improve education, to make it practical and creative and productive. In fact nothing has been done up till now.

Let the reader read with this the report of the Indian Industrial Commission recently issued under the authority of the Government of India and he will at once find the true causes which underlie the revolutionary movement in India. These causes are not in any way peculiar to Bengal or to the Punjab; they are common to the whole of India, but they have found a fruitful soil in these provinces on account of the rather intense natures of the people of these two provinces. The Bengali is an intensely patriotic and emotional being, very sensitive and very resentful; the Punjabee is intensely virile, passionate and plucky, having developed a strong, forceful character by centuries of resistance to all kind of invasions and attacks. Of the Punjab, however, we will speak later on. For the present we are concerned with Bengal only. The amazing phenomenon mentioned by the committee on p. 20 and referred to by us before is easily explained by the facts hinted in the Directors' report quoted above. And this notwithstanding the fact that in the matter of Government patronage Bengal has been the most favored province in India, throughout the period of British rule. To the Bengalis have gone all the first appointments to offices that were thrown open to the natives of the soil. They have been the recipients of the highest honors from the Government. Bengal is virtually the only province permanently settled where the Government cannot add to the Land tax fixed in 1793. The Bengalis are the people who spread over India, with every territorial extension of the British Raj. They have been the pampered and favored children of the Government and for very good reasons, too. They are the best educated and the most intelligent of all the Indian peoples. They know how to adapt themselves to all conditions and circumstances, they know how to enjoy and also how to suffer. They have subtle brains and supple bodies. The British Government could not do without them. It cannot do without them even now. Yet it was this most loyal and most dutiful, this most westernized and the best educated class which laid the foundations of the revolutionary movement and has been carrying it on *successfully* in face of all the forces of such a mighty Government as that of the British in India.

What is the reason? It is the utter economic helplessness of the younger generation, aided by a sense of extreme humiliation and degradation. The Government never earnestly applied itself to the solution of the problem. They did nothing to reduce poverty and make education practical. Every time the budget was discussed the Indian members pressed for increased expenditure on education. All their proposals and motions were rejected by the standing official majorities backed by the whole force of non-official Europeans including the missionaries. The Government thus deliberately sowed the wind. Is there any wonder that it is now reaping the whirlwind?

The cause is economic; the remedy must be economic. Make education practical, foster industries, open all Government careers to the sons of the soil, reduce the cost on the military and civil services, let the people determine the fiscal policy of the country and the revolutionary movement will subside. Die it will not, so long as there is foreign domination and foreign exploitation. Even after India has attained Home Rule it will not die. It has come to stay. India is a part of the world and revolution is in the air all the world over. The effort to kill it by repression and suppression is futile, unwise and stupid.

XIII

THE PUNJAB

We may now consider the case of the Punjab. Lord Morley's verdict notwithstanding, it is abundantly clear that the troubles of 1907, with which the history of unrest in the Punjab begins, were principally agrarian in their origin. Lord Morley's speech in the House of Commons (in 1907) as to the root of the trouble was based on reports supplied to him by the Government of the Punjab and we know from personal knowledge how unreliable many of these reports are. We may here illustrate this point by a few extracts from these documents.

(1) Lord Morley stated that: "There were twenty-eight meetings known to have been held by the leading agitators in the Punjab between 1st March and 1st May. Of these five only related, even ostensibly, to agricultural grievances; the remaining twenty-three were all purely political."

The number of meetings held from March 1 to May 1, 1907 was, at the lowest calculation, at least double of 28, or perhaps treble, and *most of them* related "even ostensibly to agricultural grievances"; the number of purely political meetings could not have exceeded ten or twelve.

(2) On p. 61 the committee writes that "Chatarji's

father too had ordered him home on discovering that he was staying with Hardayal in the house of Lajpat Rai." The whole of this statement is absolutely false. I am prepared to swear and to prove that Chatarji did not stay in my house even for a single night. He came there a few times with Hardayal. Hardayal was at that time living in a house he had rented for himself in the native city about one mile from my place which is in the Civil Station on the Lower Mall.

On the same page the committee has approvingly quoted a sentence from the judgment of the Sessions Judge in the Delhi Conspiracy Case. Speaking of Amir Chand, one of the accused in that case who was sentenced to death, the Sessions Judge describes him as "one who spent his life in furthering murderous schemes which he was too timid to carry out himself." Now I happen to have known this man for about 20 years before his conviction. I have no doubt that he was rightly convicted in this case but I have no doubt also that this description of him by the Sessions Judge was absolutely wrong. Up till 1910 the man had led an absolutely harmless life, helping students in their studies and otherwise rendering assistance, according to his means, to other needy people. No one ever credited him with violent views. His revolutionary career began in 1908. Before that he could not and would not have tolerated even the killing of an ant, much less that of human beings.

In governments by bureaucracies one of the standing formulas of official etiquette is never to question the findings of facts arrived at by your superiors or predecessors. This naturally leads to the perpetuation of mistakes. A wrong conclusion once accepted continues to be good for all times to come. The Rowlatt Committee has studiously acted on that formula throughout its present inquiry. They have invariably accepted the findings of executive and judicial authorities preceding them about the incidents that happened since 1907, without making any independent inquiry of their own. Hence their opinion about the original or the principal cause of the unrest of 1907 in the Punjab is not entitled to greater weight than that of the Punjab officials whose mishandling of the affairs of the province produced the unrest. One ounce of fact, however, is of greater weight in the determination of issues than even a hundred theories. The fact that the Government of India *had* to veto the Punjab Government's Land Colonies Act in order to allay the unrest proves conclusively that the unrest was due to agrarian trouble.

The unrest of 1907 subsided after the repeal of the land legislation of 1907, but the legacy it left is still operative.

The Sikhs and the Mussulmans of the Punjab, as well as the military classes among the Hindus, the Rajputs and the Jats, are the most virile portions of the population. They have fought the battles of the Empire. In the interests of the Empire they have travelled far and wide. Yet we find that educationally, as well as economically, they have suffered most. They have the largest numbers of illiterates among them. They are the least developed and the least progressive of all the classes in the Punjab. They are heavily in debt. The Government has occasionally recognised it and has tried to satisfy them by preferential treatment in the filling of Government posts, or in the bestowal of titles or in nominating their supposed leaders to Legislative Councils. These ridiculous palliative measures, however, have failed in their objective. The classes disaffected do not get any satisfaction by these palliative measures. They need opportunities of education and economic betterment. These could not be provided without making education general and without a more equitable distribution of land among the agricultural classes and the inauguration of industries other than agriculture. This the Government never cared to do. The Sikhs and the Mussulmans naturally directed their attention to emigration.

The opportunities they found in other parts of the Empire whetted their appetites. They compared the conditions abroad with conditions at home and drew their own conclusions. Having helped in the expansion and development of the Empire they thought they were entitled to benefit therefrom. They demanded fair treatment. Instead they found the doors shut upon them. Even those that had been admitted were made to feel the humiliation of their position. Deliberate, active, concerted measures were taken to drive them away or to make life for them intolerable. Their wives and children were refused admittance and various pretexts were invented to keep them out or to drive them away. The revolutionary movement in the Punjab amounted to nothing until it was reinforced by the return of the Sikh members of the Ghadr party during the war. The Committee has failed to answer the question: Why did the Sikhs of Vancouver and California readily fall in with the schemes of

Hardayal and Barkat Ullah, the alleged founders of the revolutionary party of California? These latter had nothing in common with the Sikhs. In language and religion, by habits and associations, they were poles apart from each other. Why did then Hardayal's propaganda find such a ready soil among the Sikhs of Vancouver B. C. We quote from the report:

"The doctrines which he preached and circulated had reached the Sikhs and other Indians resident in British Columbia. At a meeting in Vancouver in December, 1913, a poem from the Ghadr newspaper was read, in which the Hindus were urged to expel the British from India. The main grievance of the Vancouver Indians was the Canadian immigration law under which every intending Asiatic immigrant, with a few particular exceptions, has to satisfy the Canadian authorities that he is in possession of 200 dollars and has travelled by a *continuous* [1] journey on a through ticket from his native country to Canada. In 1913 three Sikh delegates visited the Punjab. They had come from America and were members of the Ghadr party who had come to reconnoitre the position. Their real purpose was recognised after their departure. They addressed meetings at various towns on the subject of the grievances of Indians in Canada and caused resolutions of protest to be passed in which all communities joined."

Again, tracing the origin of the Budge-Budge riot, the Committee remarks:

"The central figure in the narrative is a certain Gurdit Singh, a Sikh of the Amritsar district in the Punjab, who had emigrated from India 15 years before, and had for some time carried on business as a con-

[1] There never was a continuous steamer service between India and Canada.

tractor in Singapore and the Malay States. There is reason to believe that he returned to this country about 1909. He was certainly absent from Singapore for a space; and when he returned there, going on to Hong Kong, he interested himself in chartering a ship for the conveyance of Punjabis to Canada. Punjabis, and especially Sikhs, frequently seek employment in the Far East, and have for some time been tempted by the higher wages procurable in Canada. But their admission to that country is to some extent impeded by the immigration laws which we have described already.

There were already in Canada about 4,000 Indians, chiefly Punjabis. Some of these were revolutionists of the Hardayal school, some were loyal, and some had migrated from the United States on account of labour differences there. The Committee of Enquiry, which subsequently investigated the whole affair, considered that Gurdit Singh's action had been much influenced by advice and encouragement received from Indian residents in Canada. At any rate, after failing to secure a ship at Calcutta, he chartered a Japanese vessel named the *Komagata Maru* through a German agent at Hong Kong. He issued tickets and took in passengers at that post, at Shanghai, at Moji and at Yokohama. He certainly knew what the Canadian law was, but perhaps hoped to evade it by means of some appeal to the courts or by exercising political pressure. It is equally certain that many of his passengers had no clear comprehension of their prospects. The Tribunal that subsequently tried the first batch of Lahore conspirators held that probably Gurdit Singh's main object was to cause an inflammatory episode, as one of the witnesses stated that Gurdit Singh told his followers that should they be refused admission, they would return to India to expel the British. On April the 4th, 1914, the *Komagata Maru* sailed from Hong Kong. On the 23rd of May the *Komagata Maru* arrived at Vancouver with 351 Sikhs and 21 Punjabi Muhammadans on board. The local authorities refused to allow landing except in a very few cases, as the immigrants had not complied with the requirements of the law. Protests were made, and, while negotiations were proceeding, a balance of 22,000 dollars still due for the hire of the ship was paid by Vancouver Indians, and the charter was transferred to two prominent malcontents. . . . A body of police was sent to enforce the orders of the Canadian Government that the vessel should leave; but with the assistance of firearms, the police were beaten off, and it was only when a Government vessel was requisitioned with armed force that the *Komagata Maru* passengers, who had prevented their Captain from weighing anchor or getting up steam, were brought to terms. On the 23rd of July they started on their return journey with an ample stock of provisions allowed them by the Canadian Government. *They were by this time in a very bad temper as many had staked all their possessions on this venture, and had started in the full belief that the British Government would assure and guarantee their admission to a land of plenty.* This temper had been greatly aggravated by direct revolutionary influences. . . .

"During the return voyage the War broke out. On hearing at Yokohama that his ship's company would not be allowed to land at Hong Kong, Gurdit Singh replied that they were perfectly willing to go to any port in India if provisions were supplied. The British Consul at Yokohama declined to meet his demands, which were exorbitant; but the consul at Kobe was more compliant, and after telegraphic communication between Japan and India, the *Komagata Maru* started for Calcutta. At neither Hong Kong nor Singapore were the passengers allowed to land. This added to their annoyance, as, according to the findings of the Committee, many had not wished to return to India at all."

The Committee found that most of the passengers were disposed to blame the Government of India for all their misfortunes. "It is well known," states the

Report, "that the average Indian makes no distinction between the Government of the United Kingdom, that of Canada, and that of British India, or that of any colony. To him these authorities are all one and the same. And this view of the whole *Komagata Maru* business was by no means confined to the passengers on the ship. It inspired some Sikhs of the Punjab with the idea that the Government was biased against them; and it strengthened the hands of the Ghadr revolutionaries who were urging Sikhs abroad to return to India and join the mutiny which, they asserted, was about to begin. Numbers of emigrants listened to such calls and hastened back to India from Canada, the United States, the Philippines, Hong Kong and China." [The italics are ours.]

We have given this extract to show the real cause of the growth of the revolutionary movement among the Sikhs. Let the reader omit, if he can, for a moment, all references to active revolutionary propaganda and he will find that the underlying cause of this trouble was *economic*. Why did the Sikhs want to emigrate to Canada? Why did they stake all their possessions on the venture? Why were they unwilling to return to India at all? Because the economic conditions at home were so bad and the prospects abroad so good. At home their lands were not sufficient to absorb all their energies, the income was not sufficient to keep body and soul together and, in a majority of cases, what they made from land was hardly more than sufficient to pay Land Revenue to the Government and interest to the money-lender. There was nothing to bind them to their homes except the love of home land and the domestic ties. These melted away in the presence of dire necessity. In extreme need they left their homes to make more money to be able to pay their debts, to redeem their lands, if possible to purchase more land and to make life bearable and tolerable. When they came in the open world they found insurmountable barriers between them and plenty. They had helped in making the empire; the empire had enough land for all her sons and daughters; men were urgently needed to bring land into cultivation and otherwise to develop the empire; men of other races and colours were not only welcome but were being induced to come and settle by offers of all kinds. They, and they alone, were unwelcome and barred.

Add to this the attitude and the record of the Punjab Government towards political agitation and political agitators, to use their own favorite expressions. The Punjab Government was the first to resuscitate the old Regulation III of 1818 for the purpose of scotching a legitimate agitation against an obnoxious legislative measure. A wise and sagacious Government would have dropped the legislation which it was eventually found necessary to veto to maintain peace. The deportations drove the seeds of unrest deeper. The other contributory causes may be thus summed up:

(1) The Punjab Government has been the most relentless of all local governments in India in suppressing freedom of speech and press.

(2) The Punjab Government at one time was very foolishly zealous in persecuting the Arya Samajists and in making a mountain out of a molehill about the letters found in the possession of Parmanand.

(3) The sentences which the Punjab Courts have passed in cases of seditious libel are marked by such

brutality as to make them notably unique in the history of criminal administration in India.

(4) The strangulation of all open political life by direct and indirect repression led to the adoption of secret methods.

(5) The sentences passed in the Delhi Conspiracy case were much more severe than those given in Bengal in similar cases. In this case four men were hanged, two of them only because of membership in the secret conspiracy and not for actual participation in the outrage that was the subject of the charge, and two others were sentenced to seven years rigorous imprisonment each.

(6) The Budge-Budge riot and the considerable loss of life that resulted therefrom was another case of stupid management and utter incapacity to handle a delicate situation.

(7) For the Lahore Conspiracy 28 persons were hanged, and about 90 sentenced to long terms of imprisonment and transportation for life. But for the interference of Lord Hardinge the hangings would have exceeded 50. In addition some mutinous soldiers of two regiments were tried by Court Martial and a few murderous robbers and train-wreckers were dealt with by the ordinary courts. The reader may well compare this with the record of convictions relating to Bengal.

Now, we have not the slightest intention of justifying the conduct of those who conspired to overthrow the Government by force, or who committed murders, robberies or other offences in the furtherance of that design. In our judgment only madmen, ignorant of the conditions of their country, could have been guilty of such crimes. Nor are we inclined to blame the Government much for the sharp steps they took to preserve order and maintain their authority during the war. But, after all has been said, we must reiterate that the underlying causes were economic and were the direct result of Government policy.

XIV

RECOMMENDATIONS FOR REPRESSIVE LEGISLATION

THE Committee has said all that it could against individual publicists, Indian public movements and the native press. They have found no fault with the Anglo-Indian press and the Government. The whole force of their judicial acumen has been applied in recommending fresh measures of repression and suppression which they have divided into two kinds:

Punitive Measures, Permanent. (*a*) Points of General Application. The measures which we shall submit are of two kinds, viz., Punitive, by which term we mean measures better to secure the conviction and punishment of offenders, and Preventive, i.e., measures to check the spread of conspiracy and the commission of crime.

We may say at once that we do not expect very much from punitive measures.[1] The conviction of offenders will never check such a movement as that which grew up in Bengal unless all the leaders can be

[1] The Government of India have been on the inclined plane of repression as a remedy of discontent, which sometimes leads to crime, for now more than twenty years. They have in the interval placed on the Statute Book the Penal and Criminal Procedure Codes, the Post Office Amendment Acts, the Official Secrets Act, the Seditious Meetings Act, the Incitement to Offences Act, the Criminal Law Amendment Act, the Press Act, the Conspiracy Act, and the Defence of India Act. Have they attained their object? The very introduction of the two new Bills . . . is the eloquent answer. What is it but a confession of failure? . . . *Leader*, Allahabad.

convicted at the outset. Further, the real difficulties have been the scarcity of evidence due to various causes and the want of reliance whether justified or not, on such evidence as there has been. The last difficulty is fundamental and cannot be remedied. No law can direct a court to be convinced when it is not.

Punitive Measures (Permanent).

Legislation directed better to secure the punishment of seditious crime may take the shape either—

(*a*) of changes in the general law of evidence or procedure which if sound would be advisable in regard to all crime, or

(*b*) changes in the substantive law of sedition or modifications in the rules of evidence and procedure in such cases designed to deal with the special features of that class of offence.

The recommendation under (*a*) does not amount to much and we will not mention it.

Under (*b*) they recommend:

In the first place we think that a permanent enactment on the lines of Rule 25A under the Defence of India Act is required. That rule provides for the punishment of persons having prohibited documents (which may have to be defined anew) in their possession or control with (as we read the effect of the words used) intent to publish or circulate them. . . .

We also recommend that the principle of section 565 of the Code of Criminal Procedure (which provides for an order requiring notification of residence after release in the case of persons convicted a second time for certain offences) should be extended to all persons convicted of offences under Chapter VI of the Penal Code (offences against the State) whether previously convicted or not. Such persons might be ordered to give security for a period not exceeding two years for good behaviour so far as offences under Chapter VI are concerned, and in default be directed to notify their residence to Government, who should have power to restrict their movements for the period of two years after their release and prohibit them from addressing public meetings, — the term "public meetings" including in its scope political subjects as in section 4 of the Prevention of Seditious Meetings Act of 1907.

Lastly, we think that in all cases where there is a question of seditious intent, evidence of previous conviction for seditious crime or association (of an incriminating kind, of course) with persons so convicted should be admissible upon written notice to the accused with such particulars and at such a time before the evidence is given as might be fair. What we have called seditious crime would of course have to be accurately defined.

Now it is evident that after such legislation all liberty of speech and action becomes extinct. These recommendations will we fear directly lead to secret propaganda and secret action.

Under the head of emergency punitive measures the committee recommends:

Emergency Provisions for Trials. Coming now to the measures themselves, we are of opinion that provision should be made for the trial of seditious crime by Benches of three Judges without juries or assessors and without preliminary commitment proceedings or appeal. In short, the procedure we recommend should follow the lines laid down in sections 5–9 inclusive of the Defence of India Act. It should be made clear that section 512 of the Code of Criminal Procedure (relating to the giving in evidence under certain circumstances of depositions taken in the absence of an absconding accused) applies to these trials, it having, we understand, been questioned whether section 7 of the Defence of India Act has that effect.

We think it necessary to exclude juries and assessors mainly because of the terrorism to which they are liable. But terrorism apart, we do not think that they can be relied upon in this class of cases. They are too much inclined to be affected by public discussion.

We omit the detailed discussion of these provisions in which the committee has attempted to soften the sting of these recommendations by giving their reasons and by suggesting certain safeguards against their abuse. The most startling of their recommendations are however made under the head of emergency preventive measures.

Emergency Preventive Measures. We have been forced to the conclusion that it is necessary, in order to keep the conspiracies already described under control in the future, to provide for the continuance after the expiry of the Defence of India Act (though in the contingent form explained and under important limitations) of some of the powers which that measure introduced in a temporary form. By those means alone has the conspiracy been paralysed for the present and we are unable to devise any expedient operating according to strict judicial forms which can be relied upon to prevent its reviving to check it if it does revive, or, in the last resort, to suppress it anew. This will involve some infringement of the rules normally safeguarding the liberty of the subject. We have endeavored to make that infringement as small as we think possible consistently with the production of an effective scheme.

Existing Temporary Powers. The powers at present temporarily possessed by the Government are so far as material for the present purpose to be found in rules 3–7 inclusive and 12A under the Defence of India Act, 1915. We do not refer for the present to the Foreigners Ordinance, 1914, or the Ingress into India Ordinance, 1914. . . . Shortly stated, their effect is to give power to require persons by executive order to remain in any area to be specified or not to enter or remain in any such area, with penalties for breach of such requirements. These orders may be made and served on the person affected, whereupon they become binding upon him, or the person may be arrested without warrant and detained for a period not exceeding in all one month, pending an order of restriction. There is also a power of search under search warrant. It will be observed there is no provision for an examination of the cases of such persons. The decision lies solely with the Local Government. There is also the power of confinement under Regulation III of 1818.

Again:

"Two Grades of Powers Desirable. — We now proceed to elaborate . . . the scheme we suggest.

"We think, as we have already indicated, that the powers to be acquired should be of two grades capable of being called into operation separately, possibly under different forms of notification.

"The first group of powers should be of the following nature: —

"(i) to demand security with or without sureties;

"(ii) to restrict residence or to require notification of change of residence;

"(iii) to require abstention from certain acts, such as engaging in journalism, distributing leaflets or attending meetings;

"(iv) to require that the person should periodically report to the police.

"The second group of powers should be —

"(i) to arrest;

"(ii) to search under warrant;

"(iii) to confine in non-penal custody.

"In Article 196 they provide "that in respect of acts committed before the Defence of India Act expires (or an earlier date if preferred) and danger apprehended by reason of such acts in the future it should be lawful to proceed against any person under any of the provisions which we have outlined without any notification. In other words, the new law is to be deemed to be operative for that purpose immediately."

Articles 198 and 199 suggest measures for restricting "Ingress into India" and also for regulating and restricting "Inter-Provincial Movements."

Need it be said that if these recommendations are accepted there will be no liberty of press or speech in India and the Reform will fail to suppress the revolutionary movement at all. Indian opinion is unanimous in condemning these recommendations as has been proved by the unanimous opposition of all sections of Indians in the Viceroy's Legislative Council to the bills that have been introduced to give effect to them.

XV

THE REVOLUTIONARY PARTY

Revolution is a fever brought about by the constant and reckless disregard of the laws of health in the government of a country.

DAVID LLOYD GEORGE

"Causes and Aims of the War." Speech delivered at Glasgow, on being presented with the freedom of that city, June 29, 1917.

The authors of the report remark:

"There exists a small revolutionary party deluded by hatred of British rule and desire for the elimination of the Englishman into the belief that the path to independence or constitutional liberty lies through anarchical crime. Now it may be that such persons will see for themselves the wisdom of abandoning methods which are as futile as criminal; though if they do not, the powers of the law are or can be made sufficient for the maintenance of order. But the existence of such people is a warning against the possible consequences of unrestrained agitation in India. We are justified in calling on the political leaders, in the work of education that they will undertake, to bear carefully in mind the political inexperience of their hearers; and to look for further progress not to fiery agitation which may have consequences quite beyond their grasp, but to the machinery which we devise for the purpose. In every country there will be persons who love agitation for agitation's sake or to whom it appeals like an intoxicant. It is the duty of the leaders of Indian opinion to remember the effect on people not accustomed to weighing words of fiery and heated speeches. Where ignorance is widespread and passions are so easily aroused, nothing is easier than for political leaders to excite a storm; nothing harder for them than to allay it. Breaches of the peace or crimes of violence only put back the political clock. Above all things, when the future of India depends upon co-operation among all races, attacks upon one race or religion or upon another jeopardise the whole experiment. Nor can the condemnation of extremist and revolutionary action be left only to the official classes. We call upon all those who claim to be leaders to condemn with us and to support us in dealing with methods of agitation which drive schoolboys to crime and lead to religious and agrarian disturbance. Now that His Majesty's Government have declared their policy, reasonable men have something which they can oppose successfully to the excitement created by attacks on Government and by abuse of Englishmen, coupled with glowing and inaccurate accounts of India's golden past and appeals to race hatred in the name of religion. Many prominent Indians dislike and fear such methods. A new opportunity is now being offered to combat them; and we expect them to take it. Disorder must be prejudicial to the cause of progress and especially disorder as a political weapon."

We are in general agreement with the sentiments expressed in this extract but we will be wanting in candour if we fail to point out that, though the revolutionary movement in India is mainly political, it is partly economic and partly anarchic also. In the first two aspects it is at present the product of purely local (Indian) conditions. In the last, it is the reaction of world forces. While we are hoping that the change in the policy, now announced, will remove the political basis of it, we are not quite sure that that will ensure the extermination of the party or the total destruction of the movement. The growth of democratic political institutions in India must inevitably be followed by a movement for social democracy. The spirit of Revolution which is now fed by political inequalities will, when these are removed, find its sustenance in social inequalities. That movement may not be anti-British; perhaps it will not be, but that it will have some revolutionary element in it may be assumed. The lessons of history make it clear that the most effective way to prevent its falling into channels of violence is to have as little recourse to coercion as may be consistent with the preservation of general order and peace. The preservation of order and the unhindered exercise of private rights by all citizens is the pre-requisite condition to good government. Every government must see to it. It is their duty to use preventive as well as punitive methods. There are, however, ways of doing these things. One is the British, the American and the French way.[1] The other is what was heretofore associated with the name of the late Czar. The third is the German way. We hope the lessons of Czarism will not be lost on either party. The governments have as much to learn from it as the peoples. The best guarantee against the abnormal growth of a revolutionary movement is to adopt and follow the British methods and to avoid

[1] By this we do not mean those that were adopted during the war.

scrupulously and without fail any approach to the discredited Russian or Prussian methods.

The Indian soil and the Indian atmosphere are not very congenial for revolutionary ideas and revolutionary methods. The people are too docile, gentle, law-abiding and spiritually inclined to take to them readily. They are by nature and tradition neither vindictive nor revengeful. Their general spirit is opposed to all kinds of violence. They have little faith in the virtues of force. Unless they are provoked, and that too terribly, and are face to face with serious danger they do not like the use of force, even when recourse to it may be legal and morally defensible.

One of the causes of the growth of the revolutionary movement in India has been the insolence and the incivility of the European Community towards the Indian Community. The charges of cowardice so often hurled against the Bengali have played no insignificant part in the genesis of the Bengal revolutionary. The distinguished authors have put it rather mildly:

"If there are Indians who really desire to see India leave the empire, to get rid of English officers and English commerce, we believe that among their springs of action will be found the bitterness of feeling that has been nurtured out of some manifestation that the Englishman does not think the Indian an equal. Very small seeds casually thrown may result in great harvests of political calamity. We feel that, particularly at the present stage of India's progress, it is the plain duty of every Englishman and woman, official and non-official, in India to avoid the offence and the blunder of discourtesy: and none the less is it incumbent on the educated Indian to cultivate patience and a more generous view of what may very likely be no more than heedlessness or difference of custom."

We admire the dignified way in which they have addressed their advice to the educated Indian. But we hope they do not ignore that except in a few scattered instances heretofore the chief fault has lain with the ruling class. The proceedings of the Royal Commission on the Public Services of India are full of that racial swagger which the authors of this report have mildly condemned in the above extract and it is an open secret that that spirit was one of the dearly cherished articles of faith with the bureaucracy. We hope the war has effected a great change in their temper and both parties will be disposed to profit from the advice given to them in the report.

As to the duty of the educated leaders in the matter of suppressing the growth of the revolutionary movement in future, we beg to point out that all depends on how much faith the governing classes place in the professions of the popular leaders. Open public speeches and meetings appealing to racial or religious animosities have not played any important part in the development of the revolutionary spirit. It is not likely that the educated leaders will in any way consciously and voluntarily digress from the limits of reasonable criticism of Government policy, nor have they very often done so in the past. What has so far prevented the educated leaders from exercising an effective check on the growth of the revolutionary movement is their inability to associate on terms of friendship with the younger generation. This has been due partly to a false idea of dignity and partly to the fear that any association with hot-headed young men might bring discredit on them or might land them in hot water if, sometime or other, any one of their friends might do anything violent. Public speeches denouncing the revolutionary propaganda and the revolutionary activities or public condemnation of the latter in the press are good in their own way, but they are not quite effective. The revolutionist may ascribe it to fear, timidity, or hypocrisy. What is needed is that educated leaders of influence should be free to mix, socially and otherwise, with the younger generation so as to acquire an intimate knowledge of their trend of thought and bent of mind. It is in these intimate exchanges of views that they can most effectively exercise their powers of argument and persuasion and use their influence effectively. They will not succeed always, but in a good many cases they will. This cannot be done, however, unless the Executives and the Police relax their attentions toward them.

The bureaucrats' want of confidence in any Indian leader reached its limit in the attentions which the agents of the secret service bestowed on such men as the late Mr. Gokhale. It is an open secret that the secret service records have assigned a particular number to every public leader in India. Religious preachers and teachers of the type of Lala Hansraj and Lala Mûnshi Rám receive as much attention in the records as the writer of this book or Mr. B. G. Tilak or Mr. Bepin Chandra Pal. The "Servants of India" are as much the objects of solicitation on the part of the secret service men as the members of the Arya Samaj. Of course, agitators are agitators. All the great progressive souls of the world have had to agitate at one time or another in their lives. Agitation is the soul of democracy. There can be no progress in a democracy without agitation. Sir Denzil Ibbetson could pay no greater compliment to the Arya Samaj than by his remark in 1907 that, according to his information, wherever there was an Arya Samaj it was a centre of unrest. We hope the Governments are now convinced that the Arya Samaj has never been revolutionary. It is one of the most conservative, restraining forces in the social life of the country. Yet it cannot be denied that its propaganda has been and will continue to be one of the most disturbing factors in the placid waters of Indian life. The bureaucracy could not look upon it with kindness. Any attempt to persist in this kind of control or check or persecution will be fatal to the success of the appeal which Mr. Montagu and Lord Chelmsford have addressed to the public men of India in the extract given above.

In our judgment the most effective way to check the growth of the revolutionary movement is by freeing the mind of the leaders of the fear of being misunderstood if they should mix freely with the younger generation and yet fail to prevent some of them from becoming revolutionists. A revolutionary prospers on exclusiveness. Secrecy is his great ally. Cut off a young man from open, healthy influences and he will be attracted by the mystery of secrecy. Thenceforth he is doomed. After that he may be weaned only by kindness and friendliness and not by threats or persecution. Most of the youths attracted by revolutionary propaganda have proved to be quite ignorant of the real conditions of their country. No attempt has been made to instruct them in politics. They have been fed on unsound history and unsound politics. Reactionary Imperialism has harmed them more than exaggerated nationalism. They have had few opportunities of discussion with people who could look upon things in right perspective. They could not open their minds to their European teachers. In the few cases in which they did they repented. Somehow or other, the free confidential talks they had with their professors found an entry in the police records. It brought a black mark against their names, to stand and mar their careers forever. The Indian teacher and professor is afraid of discussing politics with them. So they go on unrestrained until the glamour of prospective heroism, by a deed of violence, fascinates one of them and he is led into paths of crimes of a most detestable kind. Unscrupulous advisors lead him toward falsehood, hypocrisy, treachery, treason and crime by dubious methods. One of the things they preach is that morality has nothing to do with politics. They insinuate that the violence of militarism and Imperialism can be effectively met and checked only by violence. Poor misguided souls! They enforce their advice by the diplomatic history of Europe. They forget that once a youth is led into the ways of falsehood and unscrupulousness he may as easily use it against his friends as against his enemies. If he has no scruples about killing an enemy he may have none about killing a friend. If he has no scruples about betraying the one, he may have none about betraying the other. Once a man starts toward moral degeneration, even for desirable or patriotic ends, there is no knowing whither his course might take him. The most idealistic young men starting with the highest and purest conceptions of patriotism have been known to fall into the most ignoble methods of attacking first their enemies and then their friends. When they reach that stage of moral corruption they can trust no one, can believe in the honesty of no one. Their one idea of cleverness and efficiency is to conceal their motives from everyone, to give their confidence to no one, to suspect and distrust everyone and to aspire toward the success that consists in imposing upon all.

The remedy against this lies in encouraging an open and frank discussion of politics on the part of the younger generation, with such indulgences as are due to their youth and immaturity of judgment; a systematic teaching of political history in schools and colleges; a free and open intercourse with their teachers on the clearest understanding that nothing said in discussion or in confidence will ever be used either privately or publicly against them, and an equally free and intimate intercourse with the leaders of thought and of public life in the country. These latter must be freed from the attentions of the secret service if it is intended that they should effectually coöperate in counteracting revolutionary propaganda. Besides, the younger generation must be brought up in habits of manly and open encounter with their adversaries, in a spirit of sport and fair play. Repression, suppression, and suspicion do not provide a congenial climate for the development of these habits and they should be subordinated as much as possible in the present condition of chaotic conflict between social interests and social ideals.

XVI

EDUCATION

In the previous chapters we have embodied and discussed the important parts of the Report of Mr. Montagu and Lord Chelmsford. In this chapter we give a summary of what they say about education. The statements of fact made by the two distinguished statesmen are so lucid and fair that we make no apology for copying the whole article embodying the same.

"There is, however, one aspect of the general problem of political advance which is so important as to require notice in some detail. We have observed already that one of the greatest obstacles to India's political development lies not only in the lack of education among its peoples taken as a whole, but also in the uneven distribution of educational advance. The educational policy of Government has incurred much criticism from different points of view. Government is charged with neglect, because after sixty years of educational effort only 6 per cent. of the population is literate, while under 4 per cent. of the total population is undergoing instruction. It is charged, on the other hand, with having given to those classes which welcomed instruction a system which is divorced from their needs in being purely literary, in admitting methods of unintelligent memorising and of cramming, and in producing, far in excess of the actual demands of Indian conditions, a body of educated young men whose training has prepared them only for Government service or the practice of law. The system of university education on Western lines is represented as cutting off the students from the normal life of the country, and the want of connection between primary education in the vernaculars and higher education in English is regarded as another radical defect."

The period of sixty years mentioned is evidently counted from 1858, the year in which the rule of the East India Company ceased and the Crown assumed direct responsibility for the Government of India. British rule in India however began in 1757 A.D. and the foundation of public education in India under the British might well be considered to have been laid by Warren Hastings in 1781, in which year the Calcutta Madrassa was established. For a period of almost 50 years the discussion whether the Indians should be instructed in English or not went on until it was settled in 1835 by Lord Macaulay's famous minute in favour of English and the European system. In 1824 there were 14 public institutions in Bengal imparting education on Western lines.

In the same year, i.e., in 1824, Monstuart Elphinstone formulated a similar policy for the Bombay presidency.

To the remarks made in the above quotation about the extent and kind of education imparted in India till now, the distinguished authors of the report add:

"From the economic point of view India had been handicapped by the want of professional and technical instruction: her colleges turn out numbers of young men qualified for Government clerkships while the real interests of the country require, for example, doctors and engineers in excess of the existing supply. The charge that Government has produced a large *intelligentsia* which cannot find employment has much substance in it: it is one of the facts that lie at the root of recent political difficulties. But it is only of late years and as part of the remarkable awakening of national self-consciousness, that the complaint has been heard that the system has failed to train Indians for practical work in manufactures, commerce, and the application of science to industrial life."

After making a few general observations on the so called difficulties in the way of a general spread of education "the chief needs at present" are thus pointed out:

"Primary education, as we have seen, is already practically in the hands of local bodies, but secondary education was deliberately left at the outset almost entirely to private agencies. The universities, despite their connection with Government, are largely non-official bodies with extensive powers.[1] The main defect of the system is probably the want of co-ordination between primary and higher education, which in turn reacts upon the efficiency of the secondary institutions and to a great extent confines university colleges to the unsatisfactory function of mere finishing schools. The universities have suffered from having been allowed to drift into the position of institutions that are expected not so much to educate in the true sense as to provide the student with the means of entering an official or a professional career. Thus a high percentage of failures seems to a large body of Indian opinion not so much a proof of the faultiness of the methods of teaching as an example of an almost capricious refusal of the means of obtaining a living wage to boys who have worked for years often at the cost of real hardship to secure an independent livelihood. The educational wastage is everywhere excessive;

[1] We do not accept this statement. The Government controls the policy of the universities to such an extent as virtually to make them official institutions.

and analysis shows that it is largely due to underpayment and want of proper training in the case of teachers. The actual recruits for normal schools are too often ill-prepared, and the teaching career, which in India used formerly to command respect, does not now offer adequate inducements to men of ability and force of character. The first need, therefore, is the improvement of teaching. Until that is attained it is vain to expect that the continuation of studies from the primary stage can be made attractive. But while the improvement of primary and middle schools is the first step to be taken, very much remains to be done in reorganising the secondary teachers and ensuring for the schoolmaster a career that will satisfy an intelligent man. The improvement of ordinary secondary education is obviously a necessary condition for the development of technical instruction and the reform of the university system. It is clear that there is much scope for an efficient and highly trained inspectorate in stimulating the work of the secondary schools and in helping the inspectorate of the primary schools maintained by the local bodies. We believe that the best minds in India, while they feel that the educational service has not in the past been widely enough opened to Indians trained at British universities, value the maintenance of a close connection with educationists from the United Kingdom.

"This survey of educational problems will show how much room there is for advance and improvement, and also how real the difficulties are. The defects of the present system have often been discussed in the legislative councils, but, as was inevitable so long as the councils had no responsibility, without due appreciation of financial difficulties, or serious consideration of the question how far fresh taxation for educational improvement would be acceptable. As we shall show, it is part of the political advance that we contemplate that the direction of Indian education should be increasingly transferred to Indian hands. Only so, we believe, can the stimulus be forthcoming which will enable the necessary money to be found. The weak points are recognised. A real desire for improvement exists. Educational extension and reform must inevitably play an important part in the political progress of the country. We have already made clear our conviction that political capacity can come only through the exercise of political responsibility; and that mere education without opportunities must result in serious mischief. But there is another important element. Progress must depend on the growth of electorates and the intelligent exercise of their powers; and men will be immensely helped to become competent electors by acquiring such education as will enable them to judge candidates for their votes, and of the business done in the councils. No one would propose to prescribe an educational qualification for the vote; but no one can deny the practical difficulties which make a very general extension of the franchise impossible, until literacy is far more widely spread than is the case at present Progress was temporarily interrupted by uncertainty as to the distribution of financial resources which would result from the constitutional changes; but the imminence of these has given a new importance to the question and its consideration has been resumed. We trust that impetus will thus be given to a widespread movement which will be taken up and carried forward boldly by the reformed councils."

The subject has been so fairly dealt with, the defects of the present system so frankly recognised and the need of wider dissemination of education so forcibly explained that we need add nothing.

In our judgment the circumstances and conditions under which it is proposed to transfer the direction of Indian education to Indian hands are extremely unfair. It is admitted that under the present economic conditions of the Indian people, there is little scope for further taxation. If so, there are only two ways to find money for education, (*a*) by economy in the other departments of public administration, (*b*) by loans.

The recommendation made by the Secretary of State and the Viceroy for an increase in the emoluments of the European services hardly leaves any room for (*a*). We have discussed the matter at some length in another chapter. The only other source left, then, is by incurring debt. Education is so important and so fundamental to the future progress of the country that in our judgment the ministers should feel no hesitation in having recourse to it, but the problem is so gigantic that, lacking material reduction in the cost of administration in other departments, it will be extremely difficult to meet the situation without an unreasonable increase in the public debt. Anyway, under the scheme recommended, the Government cannot divest itself of the fullest responsibility in the matter. The scheme gives no vital power to the electorates or their representatives. The authority of the Executive in the matter of appropriations remains unaffected and so long as it retains the final say in the making of the Budget, the Indian ministers cannot, handicapped by so many restrictions, be held responsible if the progress is slow.

Our views on the problem of education in India have been expressed in a separate book to which interested readers are referred.[2] We hold that it is the duty of the Government to provide free and wholesome education to every child at public cost, that education should be compulsory up to the age

[2] National Education in India.

of 18. The policy of the English Education Act of 1918 ought to be applied to India, and if it cannot be done from current funds, loans should be raised for the purpose. It is a matter which brooks of no delay. The whole future of India depends upon it. Nay, the future of humanity as a whole is affected by it. The world cannot be safe for any kind of democracy, nor can the world make progress towards a better order without the active coöperation of three hundred and fifteen million Indians forming one-fifth of the human race. Not only is the world poorer by reason of India's inability to coöperate in the work of progress but its present educational backwardness is a serious handicap to the rest of humanity going forward.

XVII

THE PROBLEM

WE have so far discussed the Report and such remarks as we have made have been by way of comment. In this chapter we propose to give in brief outline our own view of the problem.

Let us first be clear about the exact nature of the Indian problem. Political institutions are, after all, only a reflection of the national mind and of national conditions. What is the end? The end is freedom to live and to live according to our own conception of what life should be, to pursue our own ideals, to develop our own civilization and to secure that unity of purpose which would distinguish us from the other nations of the world, insuring for us a position of independence and honor, of security from within and non-interference from without. We have no ambition to conquer and rule other peoples; we have no desire to exploit foreign markets; not even to impose our "kultur" and our "civilization" on others. At present we are counted among the backward peoples of the earth mainly because we are a subject people, governed by a foreign power, protected by foreign bayonets and schooled by foreign teachers. The condition of our masses is intellectually deplorable and economically miserable; our women are still in bondage and do not enjoy that freedom which their Western sisters have won; our domestic masters, the prince and priest, are still in saddle; caste and privilege still hold some sway, yet it is not true that, taken all in all, we are really a backward people. Even in these matters we find that the difference between us and the "advanced" nations of the world is one of degree only. Caste and privilege rule in the United States as much as in India. There is nothing in our history which can be put on the same level as the lynching of Mr. Little, the deportation of Bisbee miners, the lynching of the Negroes, and other incidents of a similar nature indicative of race hatred and deep rooted colour prejudice. No nation in the world can claim an *ideal state of society*, in which everything is of the best. On the other hand, there are certain matters in which comparison is to our advantage. Even with the advance of drunkenness under British rule we are yet a sober nation; our *standards* of personal and domestic hygiene are much higher than those of the Western people; our standards of life much simpler and nobler; our social ideals more humane; and our spiritual aspirations infinitely superior. As a nation we do not believe in war or militarism or evangelism. We do not force our views on others; we have greater toleration for other people's opinions and beliefs than has any other nation in the world; we have not yet acquired that craze for possessions and for sheer luxurious and riotous life which marks the modern Pharisee of the West. Our people, according to their conceptions, means and opportunities are kindly, hospitable, gentle, law-abiding, mutually helpful, full of respect for others, and peace loving. It is, in fact, the abnormal extent in which these qualities exist that has contributed to our political and economic exploitation by others. In India capitalism and landlordism have not yet developed as fully as they have among the civilized nations of the West. The West is in revolt against capitalism and landlordism. We do not claim that before the advent of the British there was no capitalism or landlordism in India. But we do contend that, though there was a certain amount of rivalry and competition between the different castes, within the castes there was much more coöperation and fellow-feeling than there has ever been in the West. Our native governments and their underlings, the landlords, did exact a high price from the village communities for the privilege of cultivating their lands but within the village there was no *inter se* competition either between the tillers of the soil or between the pursuers of crafts. The gulf between the rich and the poor was not so marked as it is to-day in the West.

Under the British rule and since its introduction, however, things have changed considerably. Without adopting the best features of modern life, we have been forced by circumstances, political and economic, to give up the best of our own. Village communities have been destroyed; joint and corporate bargaining has given place to individual transactions; every bit of land has been separately measured, marked and taxed; common lands have been divided; the price of land and rent has risen abnormally. The money-lender who, before the advent of British rule, held an extremely subordinate position in the village community, has suddenly come to occupy the first place. He owns the best lands and the best houses and holds the bodies and souls of the agriculturalists in mortgage. The villages which were generally homogeneous in population, bound to each other by ties of race, blood and religion, have become heterogeneous, with nondescript people of all races and all religions who have acquired land by purchase. Competition has taken the place of coöperation. A country where social coöperation and social solidarity reigned at least within castes, within villages and within urban areas has been entirely disrupted and disintegrated by unlimited and uncontrolled competition. India never knew any poor laws; she never needed any; nor orphan asylums, nor old age pensions and widow homes. She had no use for organized charity. Rarely did any man die for want of food or clothing, except in famines. Hospitality was open and was dispensed under a sense of duty and obligation and not by way of charity or kindness. The survival of the fittest had no hold on our minds. We had no factories or workshops. People worked in their *own* homes or shops either with their own money or with money borrowed from the money-lender. The artisans were the masters of the goods they produced and, unless otherwise agreed with the money-lender, sold them in the open market. The necessities of life, being cheap and easily procurable the artisans cared more for quality than quantity. Their work was a source of pleasure and pride as well as of profit to them. Now everything has gone, pleasure, pride, as well as profit. Where profit has remained, pleasure and pride are gone. We are on the high road to a "distinctly industrial civilization." In fact, the principal complaint of our political reformers and free trade economists is that the British

Government has not let us proceed on that road at a sufficiently rapid pace and that, in preventing us, they have been dominated by their own national interests more than by our own good. We saw that other nations were progressing by following the laws of industrial development, and quite naturally we also wanted to prosper by the same method. This war has opened our eyes as it has opened those of the rest of the world and we have begun to feel that the goal that we sought leads to perdition and not salvation. This makes it necessary for the Indian politicians and economists to review their ideas of political progress. What are we aiming at? Do we want to rise, in order to fall? Do we want to copy and emulate Europe even in its mistakes and blunders? Does the road to heaven lie through hell? Must we make a wreck of our ship and then try salvage? The civilization of Europe, as we have known it, is dying. It may take decades or perhaps a century or more to die. But *die it must.* This War has prepared a death bed for it from which it will never rise. Upon its ruins is rising, or will rise, another civilization which will reproduce much of what was valuable and precious in our own with much of what we never had. The question that we want to put to our compatriots is, shall we prepare ourselves for the coming era, or shall we bury ourselves in the débris of the expiring one. We have no right to answer it for others, but our answer is clear and unequivocal. We will not be a party to any scheme which shall add to the powers of the capitalist and the landlord and will introduce and accentuate the evils of the expiring industrial civilization into our beloved country.

We are not unaware that, according to the judgment of some thinkers, amongst them Karl Marx, a country must pass through the capitalistic mill, before the proletariat comes to its own. We do not believe in the truth of this theory, but even if it be true we will not consciously help in proving it to be true. The existing social order of Europe is vicious and immoral. It is worm eaten. It has the germs of plague, disease, death and destitution in it. It is in a state of decomposition. It is based on injustice, tyranny, oppression and class rule. Certain phases of it are inherent in our own system. Certain others we are borrowing from our masters in order to make a complete mess. Wisdom and foresight require that we be forewarned. What we want and what we need is not the power to implant in full force and in full vigour the *expiring* European system, but power to keep out its development on vicious lines, with opportunities of gradually and slowly undoing the evil that has already been done.

The Government of India as at present constituted is a Government of capitalists and landlords, of both England and India. Under the proposed scheme the power of the former will be reduced and that of the latter increased. The Indo-British Association does not like it, not because it loves the masses of India for which it hypocritically and insincerely professes solicitude, but because in their judgment it reduces the profits of the British governing classes. We doubt if the scheme really does affect even that. But if it does, it is good so far.

The ugly feature of the scheme is not its potentiality in transferring the power into the hands of the Brahmins (the power of the Brahmin as such, is gone for good), but in the possibility of its giving too much power to the "profiteering" class, be they the landlords of Bengal and Oudh, or the millionaires of Bombay. The scheme protects the European merchants; it confers special privileges on the small European Community; it provides special representation for the landlords, the Chambers of Commerce, the Mohammedans and the Sikhs. What is left for the general tax-paying public is precious little. The authors of the scheme say that to withhold complete and immediate Home Rule is in the interest of the general masses, the poor inarticulate ryot and the workingman. We wish we could believe in it. We wish it were true. Perhaps they mean it, but our past experience does not justify our accepting it at its face value.

There is, however, one thing we can do. We can ask them for proofs by insisting on and agitating for the immediate legislative relief of the ryot and the middle classes. We should adopt the aims of the British Labour Party as our own, start educating our people on those lines and formulate measures which will secure for them *real freedom* and not the counterfeit coin which passes for it. It will require years of education and agitation but it has to be done, no matter whether we are ruled by the British or by our own property holders. We are not opposed to Home Rule. Nay, we press for it. In our judgment the objections urged against giving it at once are flimsy and intangible. The chief obstacles are such as have been created or perpetuated by the British themselves. The caste does not prevent us from having *at least* as much home rule as is enjoyed by the people of

Italy, Hungary, the Balkan States and some of the South American Republics. But if we cannot have it at once and if the British must retain the power of final decision in their hands, we must insist upon something being immediately done not only to educate the ryot but to give him economic relief. So long as the British continue to refuse to do that we must hold them responsible for all the misery that Indian humanity is suffering from.

We want political power in order to raise the intellectual and political status of our masses. We do not want to bolster up classes. Our goal is real liberty, equality and opportunity for all. We want to avoid, if possible, the evils of the class struggle. We will pass through the mill if we must, but we should like to try to avoid it. For that reason we want freedom to legislate and freedom to determine our fiscal arrangements. That is our main purpose in our demand for Home Rule.

XVIII

THE INTERNATIONAL ASPECT

THUS far we have discussed the Indian question from the internal or national point of view. But it has an international aspect also. It is said, and we hope that it is true, that the world is entering into an era of new internationalism and that the old exclusive chauvinistic nationalism is in its last gasps. This war was the greatest social mix-up known to history. It has brought about the downfall of many monarchs and the destruction of four empires. The armies of the belligerents on both sides contained the greatest assortment of races and nations, of religions and languages that were ever brought together for mutual destruction. Primarily a fight between the European Christians, it drew into its arena Hindus, Mohammedans, Buddhists, Shintos, Jews and Negroes of Africa and America.

The war has produced a revolution in Russia, the like of which has never been known. It is now said openly that the Russian Revolution had as much influence on the final *debacle* of the Central Powers as the strength of the Allies and the resources of America. The revolution has spread to Germany and Austria and threatens to engulf the whole of Europe. It has given birth to a new order of society, aglow with the spirit of a new and elevated kind of internationalism.

This internationalism must have for its foundation justice and self-determination for all peoples, regardless of race or religion, creed or color. In the new understanding between nations coöperation must be substituted for competition and mutual trust and helpfulness for distrust and exploitation of the weaker by the stronger. The only alternatives are reaction, with the certainty of even greater war in the near future, and Bolshevism.

Now, nobody knows what Bolshevism represents. The Socialists themselves are divided over it. The advanced wing is enthusiastic, the moderates are denouncing it. The Liberals and Radicals are freely recognizing that it has brought into the affairs of men a new spirit which is going to stay and substantially influence the future of the world. The stand-patters denounce it in the strongest possible terms. They calumniate it to their heart's content and move heaven and earth to exterminate it. But we feel that only radical changes in the existing order will stem its tide. The Socialists and Radicals want to make the most of it, while the Imperialist Liberals and Conservatives want to give as little as is compatible with the safety of the existing order in which they are supreme. The struggle will take some time, but that it will end in favor of the new spirit no one doubts.

The only way to meet Bolshevism is to concede rights to the different peoples of the earth now being bled and exploited. Otherwise the discontented and exploited countries of the world will be the best breeding centres for it. India must come into her own soon, else not even the Himalayas can effectually bar the entry of Bolshevism into India. A contented, self-governing India may be proof against it; a discontented, dissatisfied, oppressed India perhaps the most fertile field. We hope the British statesmen are alive to the situation.

But that is not the only way to look at the international importance of India. By its geographical situation it is the connecting link between the Near East and the Far East and the clearing house for the trade of the world. Racially, it holds the balance between the European Aryan and the yellow races. In any military conflict between the white and the yellow races, the people of India will be a decisive factor. In a conflict of peace they will be a harmonising element. Racially they are the kin of the European. By religion and culture they are nearer the Chinese and Japanese.

With 70 million Moslems India is the most important centre of Mohammedan sentiment. With Christians as their present rulers, the Hindus and Mohammedans of India are coming to realise that their best interests require a closing up of their ranks. There is no doubt that, come what may, their relations in future will be much more cordial, friendly and mutually sympathetic than they have been in the past. The Hindus will stand by their Mohammedan countrymen in all their efforts to revive the glory of Islam, and to regain political independence for it. There is no fear of a Pan-Islamic movement if the new spirit of internationalism prevails. If, however, it does not, the Pan-Islamic movement might find a sympathetic soul in India. Islam is not dead. It cannot and will not die. The only way to make it a force for harmony and peace is to recognise its potentialities and to respect its susceptibilities. The political independence of Islamic countries is the basic foundation for such a state. We hope that the statesmen of the world will give their most earnest thought to the question and sincerely put into practice the principles they have been enunciating during the war. The case of India will be an acid test.

A happy India will make a valuable contribution to the evolution of a better and more improved humanity. An unhappy India will clog the wheels of progress. It will not be easy for the masters of India to rule it on old lines. If not reconciled it might prove the pivot of the next war. A happy India will be one of the brightest spots in the British Commonwealth. A discontented India will be a cause of standing shame and a source of never ending trouble.

With a republican China in the northeast, a constitutional Persia in the northwest and a Bolshevist Russia in the not remote north, it will be extremely foolish to attempt to rule India despotically. Not even the gods can do it. It is not possible even if the legislature devotes all its sittings to the drafting and passing of one hundred coercion acts. The peace of the world, international harmony and good-will, the good name of the British Commonwealth, the safety of the Empire as such, demand the peaceful introduction and development of democracy in India.

APPENDIX A

A SYNOPSIS OF THE INDIAN INDUSTRIAL COMMISSIONERS' REPORT

A bureaucracy has the fatal tendency of perpetuating itself and of making itself indispensable. As a result, we find that the prospects and powers of the bureaucracy become more important than even the purposes for which it exists. It is a commonplace of politics that a state exists for the people comprising it, and that the servants of the state are the servants of the people. They are the tools which the body politic uses for its corporate life. Even in self-governed countries the tendency of glorifying the state and the servants of the state at the cost of the people is not uncommon, though the fact is not, or rarely, if at all, admitted in so many words. In dependencies and countries governed by a foreign bureaucracy, however, this fact is undisguisedly kept before the people and they are openly and frankly told that the powers and prospects of the servants of the government are of greater consequence and importance than the wishes and welfare of the people. This is amply illustrated by the extravagant scale on which the government of India pays its European servants and goes on adding to their privileges under all sorts of pretences and excuses. People may live or they may die for want of food, for lack of knowledge of the ordinary laws of hygiene, for lack of employment, but the bureaucrats must enjoy their princely salaries, their hill allowances, their furlough, and travelling and leave perquisites, promotions and pensions. If the cost of living increases, they must get a raise in their salaries, no matter how the increased cost of living affects the general body of the people. Besides, they must have their pensions, as their children are infinitely more important than those of the tax-payer.

We have already reproduced and discussed the recommendations of the Secretary of State for India and the Viceroy, about the European members of the Indian services. The Viceroy has only recently emphasized the importance of a substantial increase in their salaries, although there is a deficit of 20 million dollars in the budget estimates for the next year. That is an old story, however. What we are immediately concerned with are the recommendations of the Indian Industrial Commission, in favor of creating a new branch of public service divided into the inevitable Imperial and Provincial branches, for furthering the industrial development of the country. Our meaning will be clear as we proceed.

The Indian Industrial Commission was appointed by the Government of India "to examine and report upon the possibilities of further industrial development in India and to submit its recommendations with special references to the following questions: —

(*a*) whether new openings for the profitable employment of Indian capital in commerce can be indicated.

(*b*) whether, and if so, in what manner, government can usefully give direct encouragement to industrial development,

1. by rendering technical advice more freely available;
2. by the demonstration of the possibility, on a commercial scale, of particular industries;
3. by affording, directly, or indirectly, financial assistance to industrial enterprise; or
4. by any other means which are not incompatible with the existing fiscal policy of the government of India.

The tariff question was excluded from the scope of the Commission's inquiries, though it was expressed that the "building up of industries where the capital, control and management should be in the hands of the Indians" was the "special object" which the government had in view. The Government spokesman in the meeting of the Legislative Council at which the appointment of the Commission was announced further emphasized "that it was of immense importance, alike to India herself and to the Empire as a whole, that Indians should take a larger share in the industrial development of their country." He "deprecated the taking of any steps, if it might merely mean that the manufacturer who now competes with you from a distance would transfer his activities to India and compete with you within your boundaries."

The Commission has now submitted its report which has been published as a Parliamentary blue book in a bulky volume of about 500 pages including a separate lengthy note by one of the leading Indian members of the Commission. The note is, in our judgment, very valuable, as it gives the Indian point of view of the industrial problem in such a lucid and exhaustive way as to leave no room for doubt as to what articulate India thinks in the matter. The note does not express only the personal opinion of the author but the considered views of the Indian Nationalist Party.

Both the report and the note have been the source of much personal gratification to us as they corroborate and confirm to an extraordinary extent what the author said in his book "England's Debt to India," though the report is by no means free from fallacies and one-sided statements of fact and opinions.

II

In the words of the summary prefixed to the report: "The first chapters of the report deal with India as an industrial country, her present position, and her potentialities. They show how little the march of modern industry has affected the great bulk of the Indian population, which remains engrossed in agriculture, winning a bare subsistence from the soil by antiquated methods of cultivation. Such changes as have been wrought in rural areas are the effects of economic rather than of industrial evolution. In certain centers the progress of Western industrial methods is discernible; and a number of these are described in order to present a picture of the conditions under which industries are carried on, attention being drawn to the shortage and to the general inefficiency of Indian labor and to the lack of an indigenous supervising agency. Proposals are made for the better exploitation of the forests and fisheries. In discussing the industrial deficiencies of India, the report shows how unequal the industrial development of our industries has been. Money has been invested in commerce rather than industries, and only those industries have been taken up which appeared to offer safe and easy profits. Previous to the war, too ready reliance was placed on imports from overseas, and this habit was fostered by the Government practice of purchasing stores in England. India produces nearly all the raw materials necessary for the requirements of a modern community; but is unable to manufacture many of the articles and materials necessary alike in times of peace and war. For instance, her great textile industries are dependent upon supplies of imported machinery and would have to shut down if command of the seas were lost. It is vital, therefore, for the Government to ensure the establishment of those industries in India whose absence exposes us to grave danger in event of war. The report advocates the introduction of modern methods of agriculture and in particular of labor-saving devices. Greater efficiency in cultivation, and in the preparation of produce for the market would follow; labor now wastefully employed would be set free for industries and the establishment of shops for the manufacture and repair of machinery would lead to the growth of a huge engineering industry."

The summarized statements will be made more clear by the following extracts from Chapter I on rural India.

"Famine connotes not so much a scarcity or entire absence of food as high prices and a lack of employment in the affected areas. . . . The capital in the hands of the country traders has proved insufficient to finance the ordinary movements of crops and the seasonal calls for accommodations from the main financial centers are constantly increasing. This lack of available capital is one cause of the high rates that the ryot has to pay for the ready money which he needs to buy seed and to meet the expenses of cultivation. On the other hand, money is largely invested in the purchase of landed property, the price of which has risen to very high figures in many parts of the country. . . . But the no less urgent necessity of relieving the ryot from the enormous load of debt with which he has been burdened by the dearness of agricultural capital, the necessity of meeting periodic demands for rent and his social habits, has hitherto been met only to a very small extent by co-operative organization.

"The farmer, owing partly to poverty and partly to the extreme sub-division of the land, is very often a producer on so small a scale that it is practically impossible for him to take his crops to the larger markets where he can sell at current rates to the agents of the bigger firms. . . . A better market system, co-operative selling, and education are the promising remedies."

Coming to the industrial centers of the country apart from the rural areas, the report says:

"A characteristic feature of organised industry and commerce in all the chief Indian centers is the presence of large agency firms which, except in the case of Bombay, are mainly European. In addition to participating in the export and import trade, they finance and manage industrial ventures all over the country, and often have several branches in the large towns. The importance of these agency houses may be gauged by the fact that they are in control of the majority of the cotton, jute and other mills as well as of the tea gardens and the coal mines."

The general remarks about the industrial deficiency of the country will be better understood from the following extracts:

"We have already referred to the dependence of India on outside sources of sulphur and the necessity for insisting on the local smelting of her sulphide ores. In the absence of any means for producing from purely Indian sources sulphuric, nitric, and hydrochloric acids, and alkalis, our manufactures, actual or prospective, of paper, drugs, matches, oils, explosives, disinfectants, dyes and textiles are dependent upon imports which under war conditions, might be cut off. Sources of raw materials for heavy chemicals are deficient. The output of saltpeter could be raised to 40,000 tons per annum and supplementary supplies of nitrates could be produced, if necessary, from atmospheric nitrogen; but for this again, cheap electric power is needed. Salt occurs in abundance and the establishment of caustic soda manufacture, preferably by an electric process, that would also yield chlorine, is a necessary part of our chemical programme. There are available in the country, in fair quantity, many other raw materials necessary for heavy chemical manufacture, in addition to those referred to under other heads; among them may be mentioned alum, salts, barytes, borax, gypsum, limestone, magnesia, phosphates of lime and ochres. The installation of plants for the recovery of by-products in coking has recently been undertaken, but for the recovery of tar and ammonia only. The recovery of benzol and related products has so far not been attempted nor has anything been done to utilise the tar by re-distillation or other chemical treatment.

"Although India exported raw rubber valued in 1917–1918 at 162 lakhs, rubber manufacture has not been started in the country and goods to the value of 116 lakhs were imported in 1917–1918. This industry is one of those that are essential in the national interest and should be inaugurated, if necessary, by special measures.

"Though textile industries exist on a large scale, the range of goods produced is still narrow, and we are dependent upon foreign sources for nearly all of our miscellaneous textile requirements. In addition to these, the ordinary demands of Indian consumers necessitate the import of some Rs. 66 crores worth of cotton piece-goods, and interference with this source of supply has caused serious hardship. Flax is not yet grown in appreciable quantities and the indigenous species of so-called hemp, though abundantly grown, are not at present used in any organized Indian industry.

Our ability to produce and to preserve many of our foodstuffs in transportable forms or to provide receptacles for mineral or vegetable oils depends upon the supply of tin plates which India at present imports in the absence of local manufactures.

"Our few paper factories before the war stood on an uncertain basis and we are still dependent upon foreign manufacture for most of the higher qualities."

India produces enormous quantities of leather on a relatively small scale by modern processes; and the village tanner supplies the local needs only, and with a very inferior material. To obtain the quantities and standards of finished leather which the country requires, it will be necessary to stimulate industries by the institution of technical training and by the experimental work on a considerable scale.

"Large quantities of vegetable products are exported for the manufacture of drugs, dyes and essential oils, which in many cases are re-imported into India.

"The blanks in our industrial catalog are of a kind most surprising to one familiar only with the European conditions. We have already alluded generally to the basic deficiencies in our iron and steel industries and have explained how, as a result, the many engineering shops in India are mainly devoted to the repair or to the manufacture of, hitherto mainly from imported materials, comparatively simple structures, such as roofs, bridges, wagons and tanks. India can build a small marine engine and turn out a locomotive provided certain essential parts are obtained from abroad but *she has not a machine to make nails or screws, nor can she manufacture some of the essential parts of electrical machinery.*[1]

"Electrical plant and equipment are still, therefore, imported, in spite of the fact that incandescent lamps are used by the millions and electric fans by the tens of thousands. India relies on foreign supplies of steel springs and iron chains and for wire ropes, a vital necessity of her mining industry. We have already pointed out the absence of any manufacture of textile mill accessories. The same may be said of the equipment of nearly all industrial concerns. The list of deficiencies includes all kinds of machine tools, steam engines, boilers and gas and oil engines, hydraulic presses and heavy cranes. Simple lathes, small sugar mills, small pumps, and a variety of odds and ends are made in some shops, but the basis of their manufacture and the limited scale of production do not enable them to compete with imported goods of similar character to the extent of excluding the latter. Agriculturists' and planters' tools such as ploughs, *mamooties*, spades, shovels and pickaxes are mainly imported as well as the hand tools of improved character used in most cottage industries, including wood-working tools, healds and reeds, shuttles and pickers. Bicycles, motor cycles and motor cars cannot at present be made in India though the imports under these heads were valued at Rs. 187 lakhs in 1913–1914. The manufacture of common glass is carried on in various localities, and some works have turned out ordinary domestic utensils and bottles of fair quality, but no attempt has been made to produce

[1] Italics are ours.

plate or sheet glass or indeed any of the harder kinds of commercial glass, while optical glass manufacture has never even been mooted. The extent of our dependence on imported glass is evidenced by the fact that in 1913–1914 this was valued at Rs. 164 lakhs. Porcelain insulators, good enough for low tension currents, are manufactured, but India does not produce the higher qualities of either porcelain or china. . . .

"The list of industries which, though their products are essential alike in peace and war, are lacking in this country, *is lengthy and almost ominous.*[2] Until they are brought into existence on an adequate scale, Indian capitalists will, in times of peace, be deprived of a number of profitable enterprises; whilst in the event of war which renders the sea transport impossible, India's all-important existing industries will be exposed to the risk of stoppage, her consumers to great hardship, and her armed forces to the gravest danger."

In discussing the part played by Indians of all classes in the industrial development of the Country the Commission observes:

"It is obvious that the great obstacles are the lack of even vernacular education and the low standard of comfort. The higher grade of worker, the mechanical artisan, in the absence of adequate education has been prevented from attaining a greater degree of skill. He finds himself where he is, less by deliberate choice than by the accident of his obtaining work at some railway or other engineering shop, or by the possession of a somewhat more enterprising spirit than his fellows. There is at present only very inadequate provision for any form of technical training to supplement the experience that he can gain by actual work in an engineering shop, while the generally admitted need for a more trustworthy and skillful type of man is at present met by importing chargemen and foremen from abroad."

[2] Italics are ours.

In short, the industrial deficiencies of India are directly due to

(*a*) lack of education, general, scientific, and technical.

(*b*) lack of encouragement by the Government which has so far deliberately purchased most kinds of stores needed for government requirements from England.

The agricultural deficiencies are due to the same causes plus the poverty of the ryot and his inability to secure the capital necessary for improvements on reasonable terms of interest. Yet, in spite of this we find the Commission laying unwarranted emphasis upon the creation of new posts divided into Imperial and Provincial branches for Industrial, Agricultural, and scientific experts. One should have thought that the first recommendation should be the immediate inauguration of general education throughout the country with adequate provision for technical, scientific, agricultural and commercial instruction.

The industrial development of the country needs these things: (1) general education, (2) cheap capital (3) skilled labor, (4) protection against improper foreign competition. Expert advice and research are needed very much, but no amount of research or expert advice will advance the cause of industries unless the level of general intelligence has been raised and some provision made for cheap capital and skilled labor. Says the Honorable Malaviya in his separate note:

"If the industries of India are to develop, and Indians to have a fair chance in the competition to which they are exposed, it is essential that a system of education at least as good as that of Japan should be introduced in India. I am at one with my colleagues in urging the fundamental necessity of providing primary education for the artisan and laboring population. No system of industrial and technical education can be reared except on that basis. But the artisan and laboring population do not stand apart from the rest of the community; and therefore if this *sine qua non* of industrial efficiency and economic progress is to be established it is necessary that primary education should be made universal. I agree also in urging that drawing and manual training should be introduced into primary schools as soon as possible. In my opinion, until primary education is made universal, if not compulsory, and until drawing is made a compulsory subject in all primary schools, the foundation of a satisfactory system of industrial and technical education will be wanting. Of course this will require time. But I think that that is exactly why an earnest endeavor should be made in this direction without any further avoidable delay."

In support of his opinion he quotes the following pertinent observation of Mr. Samuelson:

"In conclusion, I have to state my deep conviction that the people of India expect and demand of their government the design, organization and execution of systematic technical education and there is urgent need for it to bestir itself, for other nations have already sixty years' start of us, and have produced several generations of educated workmen. Even if we begin to-morrow the technical education of all the youths of twelve years of age, who have received sound elementary education, it will take seven years before these young men can commence the practical business of life and then they will form but an insignificant minority in an uneducated mass. It will take fifteen years before those children who have not yet begun to receive an elementary education shall have passed from the age of 7 to 21 and represent a completely trained generation; and even then they will find less than half of their comrades educated. In the race of nations, therefore, we shall find it hard to overtake the sixty years that we have lost. To-morrow, then let us undertake with all our energy our neglected task; the urgency is twofold — a small proportion of our youth has received elementary education, but no technical education: for that portion let us at once organize technical schools in every small town, technical colleges in every large town and a technical university in the metropolis. The rest of the rising generation has received no education at all, and for them let us at once organize elementary education, even if compulsory."

To provide for a new department of experts on a lavish scale before making an adequate provision for general education is putting the cart before the horse. This has been pointed out in a very able article by one of our premier scientists (who has taken a leading part in the development of Indian industries) published in the *Modern Review*, Calcutta, for March, 1919.

Says Sir P. C. Roy:

"We always begin at the wrong end. I should be the last person to disparage the necessity for scientific research. The simple fact is, however, overlooked that our agricultural population, steeped in ignorance and illiteracy and owning only small plots and scattered holdings, are not in a position to take advantage of or utilize the elaborate scientific researches which lie entombed in the bulletins and transactions of these Institutes. Mr. Mackenna very rightly observes: The Famine Commissioners, so long ago as 1880, expressed the view that no general advance in the agricultural system can be expected until the rural population had been so educated as to enable them to take a practical interest in agricultural progress and reform. These views were confirmed by the Agricultural Conference of 1888. The most important and probably the soundest proposition laid down by the Conference was that it was most desirable to extend primary education amongst agricultural classes. Such small countries as Denmark, Holland and Belgium are in a position to send immense supplies of cheese, butter, eggs, etc., to England, because the farmers there are highly advanced in general enlightenment and technical education and are thus in a position to profit by the researches of experts. The peasant proprietors of France are equally fortunate in this respect; over and above the abundant harvest of cereals they grow vine and oranges and have been highly successful in sericulture; while the silk industry, in its very cradle, so to speak, namely Murshidabad and Malda, is languishing and is in a moribund condition.

"Various forms of cattle plague, e.g., render pest, foot and mouth disease, make havoc of our cattle every year and the ignorant masses steeped in superstitions, look helplessly on and ascribe the visitations to the wrath of the Goddess Sitala. It is useless to din Pasteur's researches into their ears. As I have said before, our Government has the happy knack of beginning at the wrong end. An ignorant people and a costly machinery of scientific experts ill go together.

"The panacea recommended for the cure and treatment of all these ills is the foundation or re-organization of costly bureaus and Scientific and Technical services, the latter with the differentiation of "Imperial" and the 'Provincial' Services, which are in reality hotbeds for the breeding of racial antipathies and sedition. For the recruitment of the Scientific Services the Commissioners coolly propose that not only senior and experienced men should be obtained at as early an age as possible, preferably not exceeding 25 years. What lamentable ignorance the Commissioners betray and what poor conception they have of this vital question is further evident from what they say:

"'We should thus secure the University graduate, who had done one or perhaps two years' post-graduate work whether scientific or practical, but would not yet be confirmed in specialization. We assume that the requisite degree of specialization will be secured by adopting a system whereby study leave will be granted at some suitable time after three years, service, when a scientific officer should have developed the distinct bent." In other words, secure a dark horse and wait till he develops a distinct bent! The writer of this article naturally feels a little at home on this subject and it is only necessary to cite a few instances to illustrate how, under the proposed scheme Indians will fare. At the present moment there are four young Indian Doctors of Science of British universities, three belonging to that of London. Two of them only have been able to secure Government appointments, but these only temporary, drawing two-thirds of the grade pay. One has already given up his post in disgust because he could get no assurance that the post would be made permanent. In fact, both of them have been given distinctly to understand that as soon as the war conditions are over, permanent incumbents for these posts will be recruited at "home." In filling up the posts of the so-called experts one very important factor is overlooked. As a rule, only third rate men care to come out to India. The choice lies between the best brains of India and the mediocres of England and yet the former get but scant consideration and justice. . . . The creation of so many Scientific "Imperial" services means practically so many close preserves for Europeans.' "

In the chapter dealing with Industrial and Technical training the Commission observes:

"The system of education introduced by the Government was, at the outset, mainly intended to provide for the administrative needs of the country and encouraged literary and philosophic studies to the neglect of those of more practical character. In the result it created a disproportionate number of persons possessing purely literary education, at a time when there was hardly any form of practical education in existence. Naturally, the market value of the services of persons so educated began eventually to diminish. Throughout the nineteenth century the policy of the Government was controlled by the doctrine of *laissez-faire* in commercial and industrial matters, and its efforts to develop the resources of the country were largely limited to the provision of improved methods of transport and the construction of irrigation works. Except in Bombay, the introduction of modern methods of manufacture was almost entirely confined to the European community. The opportunities for gaining experience were not easy for Indians to come by, and there was no attempt at technical training for industries until nearly the end of the century, and then only on an inadequate scale. The non-existence of a suitable education to qualify Indians for posts requiring industrial or technical knowledge was met by the importation of men from Europe, who supervised and trained illiterate Indian labor in the mills and factories that were started. From this class of labor it was impossible to obtain the higher type of artisan capable of supervisory work."

After pointing out the lamentable deficiency and comparative failure of the half-hearted measures so far taken by the Government to provide some kind of technical education the Commission makes certain recommendations for meeting the needs of the situation, which are supplemented by some pertinent suggestions made by the Honorable Malaviya in his minority report. The aforesaid summary concludes with the following paragraph:

"To sum up, the Commission finds that India is a country rich in raw materials and in industrial possibilities, but poor in manufacturing accomplishments. The deficiencies in her industrial system are such as to render her liable to foreign penetration in time of peace and to serious danger in time of war. Her labor is inefficient, but for this reason capable of vast improvement. She relies almost entirely on foreign sources for foremen and supervisors; and her intelligentsia have yet to develop the right tradition of industrialism. Her stores of money lie inert and idle.[3] The necessity of securing the economic safety of the country and the inability of the people to secure it without the co-operation and stimulation of Govern-

[3] Are there any such stores? If so, where?

ment impose, therefore, on Government policy of energetic intervention in industrial affairs; and to discharge the multifarious activities which this policy demands, Government must be provided with a suitable industrial equipment in the form of imperial and provincial departments of Industries."

APPENDIX B

A BRIEF COMPARATIVE STATEMENT OF THE PRESENT INDIAN CONSTITUTION, THE MONTAGU-CHELMSFORD SCHEME OF REFORMS AND THE CONGRESS-LEAGUE REFORM PROPOSALS.

THE PRESENT CONSTITUTION OF INDIA

Under the Government of India Act, 1915 (5 & 6 Geo. 5, c. 61).

I. THE SECRETARY OF STATE IN COUNCIL

(1) His Majesty's Secretary of State for India superintends, directs, and controls all acts relating to the government or revenues of India. He is responsible to Parliament. He or his Council has no legislative powers.

(2) The Council of India consists of 10 to 14 members, appointed by the Secretary of State for a term of seven years; and the majority of Council must sanction expenditure of revenue and certain other specified matters. In practice two of the members have been Indians since 1907.

(3) The salaries of the Secretary of State, the Under-Secretaries and the Office establishment are paid out of Indian revenues.

II. THE GOVERNMENT OF INDIA

(1) *General.*—The Governor-General of India is appointed by the Crown. He has the absolute power of adopting, suspending or rejecting measures affecting safety, tranquillity and interest of India.

(2) *Executive Council.*—The Executive Council consists of five or six ordinary members appointed by the Crown generally for five years, with the Commander-in-chief as an extraordinary member. Governor-General in Council is the supreme autocratic authority in India in all administrative matters, and it directly administers certain Imperial Departments. One member of Council is now an Indian.

(3) *Legislative Council.*—For the purpose of legislation the Council consists of all Executive members with 60 additional members, of whom only 27 are elected by specified electorates by a method of indirect election. There is separate representation for Mohammedans. The Governor-General is the President of the Council.

The members of the Legislative Council can discuss the Budget, move resolutions or ask questions, but the Executive Government is not bound thereby. In other words the Legislative has no control over the purse or the acts of the Executive.

Every act of the Legislative requires the assent of the Governor-General, and the Crown may also disallow the same. Besides in cases of emergency the Governor-General has the power to promulgate laws in the shape of ordinances, without reference to the Legislative Council, on his own initiative or on the recommendation of Provincial Governments. These ordinances to be in force for six months.

MONTAGU-CHELMSFORD SCHEME OF REFORMS

I. THE SECRETARY OF STATE IN COUNCIL

(1) His Majesty's Secretary of State to be retained, but his salary to be transferred to British Estimates.

(2 & 3) A Committee is appointed to examine and report on the present constitution of the Council of India as well as the Office establishment. (The report of the Committee is not yet made.)

(4) The House of Commons to be asked to appoint a Select Committee for Indian affairs.

(5) Control of Parliament and the Secretary of State to be modified.

II. THE GOVERNMENT OF INDIA

(1) *General.*—The Government of India to preserve indisputable authority on all matters relating to peace, order, and good Government. It is to remain fully autocratic as at present.

A Privy Council to be established in India.

(2) *The Executive Council.*—To continue as before with maximum limit removed, but the Indian element is to be increased to two members.

Government to be empowered to appoint a limited number of members (not necessarily elected) of the Legislative Council as Under-Secretaries, similar to Parliamentary Under-Secretaries in England.

(3) *Legislative Council.*—There will be two legislative Bodies. One to be called *Legislative Assembly* (with elected majority), and the other the *Council of State* (with official majority).

The Legislative Assembly is to consist of 100 members, two-thirds of whom would be elected. Of the nominated not less than one-third should be non-officials. President to be nominated by the Governor-General.

The Council of State to consist of 50 members, of whom 21 are to be elected. The Governor-General is to be the President.

Bills passed by the Assembly must also be referred to the Council of State, the differences, if any, being settled by a joint session. But in cases where the interests of peace, order and good Government, including sound financial administration, are concerned, Governor-General shall have powers to refer a Bill to the Council of State and it will become law in the form approved by the Council of State even though it is not acceptable to the Assembly.

Legislative Assembly and the Council of State may discuss the Budget, ask questions, and pass resolutions, but they are not binding on the Executive.

The Governor-General to retain his power of assenting to Acts and promulgating ordinances on his own authority. The Crown may disallow any Act.

The Montagu - Chelmsford Scheme proposes periodical (decennial) Parliamentary inquiries to revise the constitution, both for the Central and the Provincial Governments.

CONGRESS — LEAGUE REFORM PROPOSALS

I. The Secretary of State in Council

(1) The Secretary of State to be retained. But his salary to be transferred to British Estimates.

(2) The Council of India be abolished.

(3) There should be two permanent Under-Secretaries, one of whom should be an Indian. The charges of the Indian Office establishment should be transferred to British Estimates.

(4) The proposed Select Committee of the House of Commons is not objected to.

(5) The Secretary of State for India should eventually occupy the same position as the Colonial Secretary. The control of Parliament and Secretary of State be modified only with the transfer of responsibility of the Government of India to the electorate.

II. The Government of India

(1) *General.* — The Government of India shall have undivided authority in matters concerning Peace, Tranquillity and Defence of the Country; but *subject to a Statutory Declaration* of the rights of the people of India as British citizens, viz., that all Indians are equal before law, equally entitled to a licence to bear arms and to have the freedom of speech, writing, and meeting, and also the freedom of the Press, and that no one be punished or deprived of his liberty except by a sentence of a Court of Justice.

That the principle of Responsible Government should be applied to the Central Administration by dividing the subjects into (1) reserved (2) transferred. The reserved subjects to be administered by Government without popular control. The reserved subjects shall be Foreign affairs (except relations with Colonies, and Dominions), Army, Navy, and relations with Indian Ruling Princes, as well as matters affecting public peace, tranquillity, defence of the country subject to the Declarations of Rights mentioned above. All other subjects should be transferred subjects — *i.e.,* transferred to the popular control exercised by the enlarged Legislative Assembly.

There should be no Privy Council.

(2) *Executive Council.* — The Executive Council shall consist partly of Ministers, from the Elected members of the Legislative Council, and in charge of the transferred subjects; and other members nominated by the Government in charge of the reserved subjects. When there are two or more members in charge of the reserved subjects, half the number shall be Indians.

3) *Legislative Council.* — There should be no Council of State, but only one Legislative Assembly composed of 150 members, four-fifths of whom should be elected directly by the people. The Franchise should be as broad as possible without distinction of sex, but with a proportional and communal representation for Mohammedans as settled at Lucknow. The Assembly should have an elected President. (The Moslem League does not object to the Council of State if at least half the members thereof would be elected).

The Legislative Assembly should have the same measure of fiscal autonomy as Self-Governing Dominions, and should control the Budget, excepting the reserved subjects, the allotment for which shall be a first charge on the Revenues. All Bills must be introduced and passed in the Assembly.

Provided that in the case of reserved subjects if the Legislative Assembly does not pass measures desired by Government, the Governor-General in Council may provide for the same by regulations. Such regulations will remain in force for one year, and shall not be renewed unless 40 per cent (two-fifths of the members) of the Legislative Assembly present and voting are in favour of them.

The Governor-General to retain his existing power of making ordinances and the Governor-General in Council the power of passing regulations. The Governor-General and the Crown to have also power of assent, reservation or disallowance.

The Congress — League scheme objects to periodical Commissions for revising the Constitution, and asks for a Statutory declaration that the transfer of responsibility should be completed in a period not exceeding 15 years, when India should be placed on a footing of equality with the other self-governing parts of the Empire.

III. The Provincial Governments

(1) *General.* — India, including Burma, is divided into 14 provinces, each of which has its own Provincial Government.

By a system of decentralisation, revenues are allotted to all these provinces by the Government of India. The Provincial Governments administer, under the general supervision of the Central Government, without being responsible to the Local Legislatures in any way.

(2) *Executive.* — Bombay, Bengal, and Madras have each a Governor sent from England and three (one of whom is, in practice, an Indian) Executive Councillors appointed by the Crown, with a Legislative Council.

Bihar and Orissa governed by a Lieutenant-Governor with Legislative and Executive Councils; United Provinces, Punjab and Burma by a Lieutenant-Governor with only a Legislative Council; Central Provinces and Assam by a Chief Commissioner with only a Legislative Council, and the remaining by Chief Commissioners without any Councils.

(3) *Legislative.* — The Provincial Legislative Councils enjoy limited powers for legislation in the provinces. The Governor is the President of the Council.

The elected members of the Legislative Council are elected by constituencies formed of Municipal and Local Boards, and Landlords with a separate constituency for Mohammedans. They are in a minority except in Bengal, where they have at present only a small majority. The Legislative Councils have no control over the Executive or the Budget.

The Acts of the Provincial Legislature must be assented to first by the Governor, Lieutenant Governor, or the Commissioner as the case may be, and then by the Governor-General subject always to disallowance by the Crown.

Public Services

Recruitment, examination, and other matters relating to Indian services are at present under the control of the Indian Government and the Secretary of State, with no statutory limit for recruitment in India.

Local Self-Government

Half the members of Municipalities and Local Boards are generally elected, but the bodies are under official control.

III. The Provincial Governments

(1) *General.* — All Provinces having Legislative Councils at present (except Burma) should have a Governor with Executive and Legislative Councils. A complete separation will be made between Indian and Provincial Revenues. Provincial Governments are to have certain powers of taxation and borrowing.

Responsible Government is to be introduced in the Provinces by a division of departments into reserved (for Government) and transferred (to popular control) subject to a revision after five years. (A Committee is appointed to settle which subjects should be transferred. The report is not yet out.)

(2) *The Executive* would be a kind of Diarchy, consisting of the Governor and two members (one of whom is to be an Indian) who will be in charge of the reserved subjects, and responsible only to Government; and a Minister or Ministers, nominated by the Governor from the elected members of the Council, who will be in charge of the transferred subjects and responsible not to the Legislature, but to the electors who may not elect him next time. There may also be additional members without Portfolios for the purpose of consultation.

Ministers to have no voice in decisions concerning reserved subjects or about the supply for them in the Budget.

There will be Under-Secretaries and Standing Committees from the members of the Legislative Councils to assist the Executive.

(3) *Legislative Councils.* — These would be practically two Provincial Legislative Bodies: (1) Legislative Council. (2) Grand Committee.

The Legislative Council will have a substantial elected majority, elected on a broad franchise with Governor as President. (A Commission is appointed to inquire into the question of franchise and the composition of the Council, but the report is not yet out.)

The Grand Committee will comprise only from 40 to 50 per cent of Legislative Council, and its members will be partly elected by a ballot and partly appointed by nomination.

All Legislation and the Budget for transferred subjects only must be passed in the Legislative Councils.

But when the Governor certifies that a bill dealing with reserved subjects is essential he may refer the Bill to the Grand Committee and have it finally passed there.

The members of the Legislative Council can ask questions and pass resolutions, but the latter are not binding on the Executive, except resolutions on the Budget for the transferred subjects.

All Provincial Legislation requires the assent of the Governor and the Governor-General, and is also subject to disallowance by His Majesty.

Public Service

Racial bars should not exist. In addition to recruitment in England a system of appointment to all public services be established in India with an increasing percentage of recruitment. In the case of Indian Civil Service the percentage should be 33 of the superior posts, with annual increment of $1\frac{1}{2}$ per cent.

Local Self-Government

Complete popular control in Local Bodies to be established as far as possible.

III. The Provincial Governments

(1) *General.* — There should be a complete separation of the Provincial from the Imperial Revenues. All Provincial Governments should have certain powers of taxation and borrowing.

(2) *Executive.* — Full responsible Government should be introduced into the Provinces. The Executive will thus consist of the Governor and Ministers responsible to the Legislature. There should be no distinction of transferred or reserved subjects.

(3) *Legislative.* — There should be only one Legislative Council, having four-fifths of its members elected on a broad franchise without distinction of sex, but with a proportional and communal representation for the Mohammedans. The Legislative Council should elect its own President, and must have control over the Budget. All Bills must be introduced and passed in this Legislative Council.

The Governor to retain his power of assent, and the Governor-General and the Crown the power of assent or disallowance.

Public Services

Services should be recruited in India in a fixed and progressive proportion. The annual recruitment in India for the Indian Civil Service should be 50 per cent to start with, and that Indians be granted at least 25 per cent of the Commissions in Army and the proportion be gradually increased. There should be no racial distinctions.

Local Self-Government

Municipal and Local Bodies should be completely under popular control.

APPENDIX C

REPORTS OF COMMITTEES ON FRANCHISES AND DIVISION OF FUNCTIONS

(*London Times* May 13, 1919)

The reports of the two Committees which sat in India from early in November to the end of February last to fill out the framework of the Montagu-Chelmsford Report published last July were issued last night.

The Franchise Committee, of which Lord Southborough was chairman, recommend a scheme of territorial constituencies, urban and rural, the latter based on the existing land revenue districts, together with communal representation for Mohammedans and Sikhs (as contemplated in the original scheme) and for Indian Christians, Europeans, and Anglo-Indians: and the representation of special interests, including commerce and industry.

The other Committee, of which Mr. R. Feetham was chairman, make detailed recommendations as to the division of functions between the Government of India and the provincial Governments, and also between "reserved" and "transferred" subjects in the provinces. Proposals are made for the modification in some important respects (notably in the powers conferred on the Governor) of the "diarchial" system in the provinces set forth in what is conveniently called the "Joint Report."

As was indicated in *The Times* on April 5, Lord Southborough's Committee have not accepted the appeals addressed to them in the interest of woman suffrage. They found it advocated "rather on general grounds than on considerations of practicability." They are satisfied that the social conditions of India would make such a step now premature. They are of opinion, however, that at the revision of the constitutions of the councils proposed in the Joint Report 10 years after their reconstitution the matter should be reconsidered in the light of the experience gained and of social conditions as they then exist.

Franchise Qualifications

The general proposals for the franchise are based upon the principle of residence and the possession of certain property qualifications. In addition the enfranchisement of all retired and pensioned officers of the Indian Army, whether of commissioned or non-commissioned rank, is recommended. This step was universally and strongly recommended in the Punjab, and it is to extend to all provinces. The property qualification is adapted to local conditions and is guided by the principle that the franchise should be as broad as possible, consistently with the avoidance of any such inordinate extension as might lead to a breakdown of the machinery of election through weight of numbers. The large proportion of illiterate voters, in the absence of a literary test, may cause difficulty, but it has already been faced successfully in municipal elections in India by the use of coloured ballot-boxes and other like devices.

No rigid uniformity of property qualification has been sought, but the committee have proposed the same qualification for all communities within the same area. A substantially higher proportion of the urban than of the rural population will be enfranchised. At present the total number of electors for the provincial councils is 33,007, and of these no fewer than 17,448 are Mohammedans, since that community enjoys direct representation on an individual basis. The number of voters will be raised under the scheme to 5,179,000, being 2.34 per cent of the total population in the eight provinces, which is nearly 220,000,000.

The long established administrative unit of the "district" is made the territorial area for constituencies but the relatively few cities with large populations are to be separately represented. Occasionally towns are grouped into separate urban constituencies. Single-member constituencies are the general rule, but latitude is left to the local Governments. Plural voting is to be forbidden, but this does not apply to electors in constituencies formed for the representation of special interests.

Special Communities

In conformity with the recognition of the Joint Report that separate Mohammedan representation cannot be abandoned, the scheme provides for Mohammedan constituencies. The compact of the joint session of the National Congress and the Moslem League at Lucknow in December, 1916, is accepted as a guide in allocating the proportion of Mohammedan seats. In the Punjab this facility is to be extended to the Sikhs. Beyond this the framers of the

Joint Report did not propose to go; but Lord Southborough's Committee recommend separate electorates, where the numbers justify that course, for Indian Christians, Europeans, and the domiciled "Anglo-Indians"—*i.e.*, country-born Europeans and Eurasians. It is observed that candidates belonging to these communities would have no chance of being elected by general constituencies. The hope is expressed that it will be possible "at no very distant date to merge all communities into one general electorate."

Other claims for separate electorates are not conceded. Regret is expressed that the organized non-Brahmans of the Madras Presidency refuse to appear before the Committee. It is pointed out that there the non-Brahmans (omitting the depressed or "untouchable" classes) outnumber the Brahmans by about 22 to one; and on the basis of enfranchisement taken in Madras the non-Brahmans would be in the proportion of four to one. It is held to be unreasonable to adopt the proposed expedient for a community which has an overwhelming electoral strength.

The alternative of reserving a considerable number of seats for non-Brahmans in plural member constituencies did not commend itself to a section of the non-Brahmans, though evidence went to show that such a proposal might be accepted by the Brahmans "if it were the price of an enduring peace." It is suggested that his Majesty's Government might afford the parties to the controversy an opportunity, before the electoral machinery for the Presidency is completed, of agreeing upon some solution—*e.g.*, the provision of plural member constituencies and of a certain proportion of guaranteed non-Brahman seats.

The separate representation of zamindars and landholders granted under the Morley-Minto scheme is extended and provision made for university seats. The election by accredited bodies of representatives of commerce and industry is also continued and amplified. There is to be nomination for the representation of the "depressed classes," for in no case was it found possible to provide an electorate on any satisfactory system of franchise. Labour is to be represented by nomination where the industrial conditions seem likely to give rise to labour problems. The majority of the Committee are of opinion that dismissal from Government service should constitute a bar to candidature if it has taken place in circumstances which, in the opinion of the Governor in Council, involve moral turpitude; but Lord Southborough, Mr. S. N. Bannerjea, and Mr. Sastri dissent, considering it improper to limit the choice of the electorate by a disqualification based on the decision of an executive authority.

The size of the Provincial Legislatures will vary from 53 in Assam to 125 in Bengal. The eight Councils will comprise 796 members, made up as follows:—

Elected by general constituencies, 308.

By communities, 185,

By landholders, 35.

By universities, 8.

By commercial, industrial, and planting interests, 45.

The nominated representatives will number 47, and the officials, 128.

The "All-India" Body

For the Indian Legislative Assembly, the Committee propose 80 elected members, instead of the 68 suggested in the Joint Report. Fourteen representatives appointed by nomination and 26 officials (including seven *ex-officio* members) will bring up the total, exclusive of the Governor-General, to 120, as compared with 68 at present. A statement of the manifold difficulties in the way of direct election for this All-India body leads to the conclusion that there must be indirect election for all general and communal seats by the members of the Provincial Legislatures. "We trust that, in progress of time, a growing sense of political organization will enable indirect election to be superseded by some direct method."

A scheme for the creation of the "Council of State" on the lines of the Joint Report is set forth, on the basis of election thereto by non-official members of the Provincial Councils. There would be 24 elected and 32 *ex-officio* or nominated members, exclusive of the Governor-General. The electors should be left free to choose any person qualified to be a member of a Provincial Legislature.

THE DIVISION OF FUNCTIONS

The first duty of Mr. Feetham's Committee was to consider what were the services to be appropriated to the provinces, all others remaining with the Government of India. The Committee proceeded on the basis that there is to be no such statutory demarcation of powers as to leave the validity of Acts passed to be challenged in the Courts. In other words, no alteration is proposed in the system under which the All-India Legislature as regards British India, and each of the Provincial Legislatures as regards its own province, have in theory concurrent jurisdiction over the whole legislative field.

In framing the lists the Committee have treated as All-India subjects certain large general heads, such, for instance, as commerce and laws regarding property, but have taken out of these and allotted to the provinces important sections — *e.g.*, in the case of the first Excise, and in the case of the second laws regarding land tenure. Any matter included in the provincial list is to be deemed to be excluded from any All-India subject of which otherwise it would form part. Subjects not expressly included in either list are regarded as All-India subjects, but the Governor-General in Council may add to the provincial list "matters of merely local or private interest within the province." It is claimed that the scheme has been devised on such a basis as to leave the way open for the process of development.

The list of subjects to be transferred to Indian Ministers is on the whole more extensive than the suggested list attached to the Joint Report. With certain reservations University education is to be transferred, as well as primary, secondary, and technical, on the ground that the educational system must be regarded as an organic whole. But European and Anglo-Indian education, which is organized on a separate basis is excluded from the transfer.

The decision of the functions of the Provincial Government, popularly known as diarchy, has been criticized as likely to lead to friction, and sometimes to deadlock. To mitigate these difficulties, the Committee propose important changes in the relations of the Governor with both sections of the Government. It is to be the duty of the Governor in Council in the case of reserved departments, and of the Governor and Ministers in the case of transferred departments, to take care that the administration is so conducted as not to prejudice or occasion undue interference with the working of any department falling in the other category. The Governor has to decide whether a particular matter falls within the scope of a reserved or a transferred department, and to take care that any order given by the Governor-General in Council is complied with by the department concerned.

Governor's Increased Powers

In the case of disagreement between the Executive Council and Ministers as to action which appears to the Governor to affect both a reserved and a transferred department, the Governor is to give such decision as the interests of good government may seem to require, provided that, in so far as circumstances admit, before such decision is given the matter should be considered by both sections of the Government sitting together. If the Minister remains obdurate, it will be for the Governor to dismiss and find another Minister.

If, owing to a vacancy, there is no Minister in charge of a transferred department, the Governor will certify that such emergency exists and that immediate action is necessary. On such certificate being given, the Governor in Council will have authority to take action, subject to the obligation of reporting to the Governor-General in Council. In other words there will be re-entry for a temporary and limited purpose during an interregnum. This is a considerable departure from the proposal of the Joint Report that Ministers shall hold office for the lifetime of the Legislative Council. The power of the Governor to dismiss a Minister, says the report, "seems essential if deadlocks are to be avoided." The over-ruling of a minister will depend in the last resort on the Governor's personal judgment of the situation.

Finance

The Committee felt themselves precluded from considering any modification of the proposals of the Joint Report for the separation of the finances of the Government of India and of Provincial Governments. No opinion is expressed on memoranda received at a late stage from Sir James Meston making proposals for substantial departure from the plan of dealing with provincial finance set forth in the Joint Report.

It may be recalled that Mr. Montagu and Lord Chelmsford proposed that, if the residue of the provincial revenues is not sufficient, it should be open to Ministers to suggest fresh taxation. The Committee take the view that when any new provincial tax or any proposed addition to an existing tax requires legislation to give effect to it, the decision whether that legislation should be undertaken must rest with the Governor and Ministers. Since the whole balance of the revenues of the province will be at the disposal of the Ministers for the administration of the transferred departments, the Committee consider that when an existing tax cannot be reduced or remitted without legislation, the decision whether legislation should be undertaken must also rest with the Governor and Ministers. To that extent taxation for provincial purposes should be regarded as a transferred subject.

The assessment or collection of the tax would be reserved or transferred, according as the agency employed belonged to a reserved or to a transferred department. The view is also taken that, when alterations in taxation can be effected without any change in the law, the decision whether any alteration should in fact be made must be recognized as resting with the Governor in Council if the department is reserved, and with the Governor and Ministers if it is transferred.

In respect to the powers of borrowing on the sole credit of provincial revenues which are to be conferred, the Committee propose that, if after joint deliberation there is a difference of opinion between the Executive Council and the Ministers, the final decision whether a loan should be raised and as to the amount of the loan must rest with the Governor.

The Public Services

Detailed proposals are made in relation to the public services, to be classified as Indian (All-India), provincial and subordinate, No service is to be included in the first of these categories without the sanction of the Secretary of State, while the demarcation between the provincial and subordinate services is to be left to the provincial Governments.

General approval is given to a scheme prepared by the Government of India providing that legislation should be undertaken in Parliament to declare the tenure and provide for the classification of the public service. It should secure the pensions of the All-India services, and should empower the Secretary of State to make rules for their conduct and rights and liabilities, and to fix their pay and regulate their allowances. Similar legislation should be passed by the Government of India in respect to the provincial services, and to empower the provincial Governments to make rules for the subordinate services. The Committee does not express any opinion on the proposal of the Government of India to set up a statutory Public Service Commission on lines somewhat wider than those of the Civil Commission in Great Britain.

Among the clauses suggested for insertion in the instructions for each provincial Governor is one enjoining him to "protect all members of the public services in the legitimate exercise of their functions and enjoyment of all recognized rights and privileges."

The instructions are to charge him with the duty of safeguarding the legitimate interests of the Anglo-Indian or domiciled community, and "to take care that no change in educational policy, affecting adversely Government assistance afforded to existing institutions maintained or controlled by religious bodies, is adopted without due consideration." The Governor is also to be instructed that he "shall not sanction the grant of monopolies or special privileges to private undertakings which are inconsistent with the public interest, nor shall he permit any unfair discrimination in matters affecting commercial or industrial interests."